# THE SNAKE IN THE SANDTRAP

# THE SNAKE IN THE SANDTRAP

## AND OTHER TALL TALES

# LEE TREVINO

## WITH SAM BLAIR

*Illustrations by Jake Tebbit*

**STANLEY PAUL**

London Melbourne Sydney Auckland Johannesburg

Stanley Paul & Co. Ltd.

An imprint of Century Hutchinson Ltd

62–65 Chandos Place, London WC2N 4NW

Century Hutchinson (Australia) Pty Ltd
16–22 Church Street, Hawthorn, Melbourne, Victoria 3122

Century Hutchinson (NZ) Ltd
32–34 View Road, Glenfield, Auckland 10

Century Hutchinson (SA) Pty Ltd
PO Box 337, Bergvlei 2012, South Africa

First published in the USA by Holt, Rinehart and Winston 1985
First published in Great Britain 1986
© Lee Trevino and Sam Blair 1986
Illustrations © Jake Tebbit

Set in Linotron Century by Input Typesetting Ltd, London
Printed and bound in Great Britain by Anchor Brendon Ltd,
Tiptree, Essex

British Library Cataloguing in Publication Data

Trevino, Lee
The snake in the sandtrap and other tall tales.
1. Golf—Anecdotes, facetiae, satire, etc.
I. Title    II. Blair, Sam
796.352    GV967

ISBN 0 09 162250 6

# CONTENTS

# OF DRIVES AND WIVES

When it comes to the game of life, I figure I've played the whole course. I've been struck by lightning and I've managed to make a few million dollars, although I never reached the eighth grade in school. There are certain special things in this world and right at the top are drivers and wives. I know. I've had three of each.

And from all this experience I've learned that a good driver is a helluva lot harder to find than a good wife.

A driver is the key to the golf round – the key that starts your car, the key that opens your house. Without a good driver, you're not going to put the ball down in the middle of the fairway.

Unless you have a good wife, you're always going to wonder where she is and what she's doing. Same thing with a driver. If it's not working right, when you stand over it you always wonder where the ball is going.

I mean this as no offence to my lovely wife, Claudia, a young lady who booted me in the rear and got me to play the way I should. 1984 was our first year of marriage and what a year it was! I was forty-four and mentioned that maybe my age was a problem out there. Well, she looked me in the eye and said, 'Those clubs don't know how old you are.'

She was right. In August I won the PGA (Professional Golfers' Association Tournament), my sixth major championship but my first in ten years. She was twenty-five when we married in December 1983, her dad was a club pro in Connecticut and she's known golf all her life. She understands what I'm saying about the driver.

My first wife, Linda, didn't even understand why I spent most of my time playing at Tenison Park in Dallas when I wasn't working at Hardy's Driving Range. She called me a golf bum. That marriage lasted two years.

My second wife, also named Claudia, didn't know anything about golf when we met but later she started playing some. She was excited about my success as a professional golfer during our early years but toward the end, after seventeen years of marriage, she wasn't too thrilled with my career.

I know I made some mistakes through the years. One was lending her my driver.

That was the Wilson driver I used when I won my first US Open in 1968. I loved how I could hit a little banana with it from left to right out there in the middle of the fairway. We lived in El Paso then, and when I was home later that summer she and I played in a pro-am match at the Fort Bliss golf course. It was a shotgun start; we began on the 17th tee. When we finished at 16, we had a big gallery, so we decided to play 17 and 18 again just for fun.

She said, 'They've taken my clubs in. Let me hit your driver.' She took a swing with it, caught the ball in the heel of the driver and the damn thing exploded. I mean it disintegrated. All that was left was the shaft with the screw that sticks into the clubhead. I took it and chased her all the way to the clubhouse.

I went through a couple of years where I had a difficult time finding another driver just like it. It never occurred to me the reason that driver was so good was because of the shaft. I had thrown it away and started looking for another driver. I should have looked for another good driver and put that old shaft in the new clubhead. Then I would have had a duplication.

Finally in 1970 I found a MacGregor driver I really liked and I used it for many years. It was a 1960 model that had a little nickel insert in the face. I won a lot of tournaments with that driver, including another US Open, a couple of British Opens, and my first PGA Championship. Finally, that insert came apart. I took the driver to a good golf repair shop and they replaced the insert, but I didn't feel right with it after that. I lost confidence in it. Subconsciously, I knew it wasn't the same driver.

It was the same shaft, same weight. Everything was exactly the same, but I was never able to hit that thing again.

That's when I went to the metal driver. I started hitting the ball longer than I ever had, and I was putting it where I wanted it in the fairways, but I still played hot and cold. Then my new wife set my head straight.

We were playing the Tournament Players Championship at Sawgrass

in Florida, a course that has been heavily criticized since it was built a few years ago. I shot a 76 the first round, when the wind was bad and everything was difficult. I felt pretty low that night. The second day the wind calmed down, the sun was shining, and I shot a 66.

She had never seen the course until I played those two rounds, but she knew enough about golf to tell me something very important.

'Don't ever tell me again that you're through and can't play,' she said. 'For any man who can shoot a 66 on that abortion, the other golf courses have to be a piece of cake.'

That really inspired me. The next day I shot 69 and moved into the top ten on the leader board. The last round I shot 67 and made up 4 strokes on the leader, Fred Couples. I finished second, 1 shot behind him, and I felt I should have won. But I really was encouraged after playing the last three rounds 14 under par. And I won $86,000 for a second.

So we went on from there and, thanks to her, I had a better attitude about playing than I'd had in years. Hey, I trust that lady. I trust her with my life. I even trust her with my driver.

# GRINS ON THE GREENS

For years if I had been asked to rank the Masters on a scale of one to ten I probably would have given it a zero. Now I believe I can win it.

And I'm going to put on my space suit and go play the back nine on the moon, right?

Hey, I'm serious. I'm cold sober. I don't smoke those funny cigarettes. I just found a new putter, that's all.

Because of that, I should have a real chance at the Augusta National. It's just a putting contest there. That's how Ben Crenshaw won in 1984.

Ben is the nicest guy in the world but he can't keep his ball on the fairway. I've told him that he might have a tan like mine if he didn't spend so much time in the trees. He can't hit it straight, but Augusta is so wide open that he has a lot of room for error there. And he can putt.

When they slipped one of those green Masters champion's jackets on Ben I was very happy for him. But I was a lot happier a few months later when I found out what was wrong with my putting.

We played the British Open at St Andrews the following July, and I was high on the leader board after 36 holes but feeling a little uneasy about it. Even though I shot 70 and 67 I really didn't putt all that well. I just hit the ball so close that I couldn't miss the holes.

Then I went out in the third round and shot 75, with 35 putts. In the fourth round I hit the ball as well as I had any other day at the British Open, but I had 36 putts and shot 73. Seve Ballesteros won with 276, and I was 9 shots back.

I knew I had a problem but I couldn't figure it out. I was putting with my regular blade putter, an 8802 I had used since 1977.

I went down to Birmingham to play an exhibition with Seve, Nicky

Faldo, and Brian Waites. Same story. Then we went to the Dutch Open and I shot 74, with 36 putts.

Claudia was waiting for me when I came off the 18th green. I walked toward her, held that putter out and began humming taps: *Da-dada, da-dada. . . .* 'Let's dig a little hole and bury it,' I said. 'This is an old soldier. It's won many battles. It's lost a few, too, and now it's tired.'

It seemed that players winning all the money were using Ping putters, but I had no idea why. I decided to buy one and see what I could do with it. I went into the pro shop and they had one, and it had A BLADE stamped on it. It was upright. It had some loft on it. It looked ugly but that's all there was. I paid $50 for it, took it right out on the putting green, and didn't even make a putt.

'Well, maybe things will get better,' I said, and we went back to our hotel. Our room had concrete under the carpet, so I took that new putter and hit it on the floor on the heel of the putter as hard as I could. That flattened it – just the way I like it.

Then it had too much loft on it, so I put it on the floor face down and kicked it in the hosel with my heel. That took the loft off it. Now it looked pretty good.

Well, I went out the next three days and shot 14 under par with that putter, using the same stroke and hitting the ball the same way. Back in the US I played in a 36-hole benefit at Erie, Pennsylvania, and shot 13 under par. We went to Michigan for the Buick Open and I was 22 under for the week, including the pro-am, and shot a course-record 64 in the second round.

Then at Shoal Creek near Birmingham, Alabama, I became the first player ever to win the PGA Championship with four rounds in the 60s. My winning score of 273 was 15 under par and beat the record Hal Sutton set the year before by 5 strokes. Since walking out of that pro shop at the Dutch Open with my Ping putter, I was 64 under par for fourteen rounds. By then, I wouldn't have taken $50,000 for it.

Why that putter and not any of the others? Well, eight of the top ten finishers in the British Open used a Ping, and there had to be a reason for it. I understood a lot better after Seve Ballesteros demonstrated something to me I'd never seen before.

He made me put a ball right in the heel, stroke it on that heel, and hit it 20 feet. The ball went exactly where I was looking 20 feet away. Then he told me to put a ball in the middle of the face of the putter and

hit it 20 feet, and it did the same thing. Then he told me to putt a ball off the extreme toe of it, and it also went 20 feet.

Seve said, 'It makes no difference where you hit the ball on the face of the putter. It still will go the distance that you're playing for.' And that's exactly what happened for me, time after time.

I slept like a baby the night before that last round in the PGA. I led Lanny Wadkins by 1 and Gary Player by 2, and a lot of people favoured Lanny to win. He's ten years younger than I am, fourteen years younger than Gary, and he's a helluva player. But I was confident. I had been driving the ball well for months, and now I had that putter working for me. Feeling that kind of confidence, I went for the flag. I never let up. I wasn't scared to chip out of the rough. I wasn't scared of any 6- or 8- or 10-foot putt. I felt I was going to make them.

The first hole didn't hurt that confidence any. I was looking at a 60-foot putt, a big curver going up the hill, and I knocked it in dead. 'Wait a minute,' I told myself. 'This is it!'

Lanny is a battler, though, and after 10 he had a 1-shot lead. But I pulled even on 11 when he made a 6, and I went 1 shot up on him when he 3-putted 12. Then on 14 I sank an 8-foot birdie putt and went 2 up. Lanny birdied 15 and cut it to 1 again. I was in trouble on 16, and Lanny might have taken the lead again if I hadn't made it up and down from a bunker. I chipped 15 feet past the cup and then made my putt to save a par while Lanny was waiting to putt from 10 feet. So I went to 17 with my 1-shot lead intact, and the heat was on Lanny.

He missed a 35-foot putt by inches and bogeyed 17, and I led by 2. Then he bogeyed again on 18 and I won by 4 when I knocked in a 15-foot birdie putt.

I felt so confident when I stood over that last putt that I didn't even line it up. I didn't realize I was setting a scoring record, that I was the first ever to shoot four rounds in the 60s in the PGA, or that my prize money would be $125,000. I just drew my putter back, hit the ball, and made the putt. Then I thought, 'Now what do I do?'

I was too old to jump. I can jump as high as I ever could, but I can't stay up as long. I didn't want to throw my cap in the air, because it wasn't mine. I forgot my own cap that morning and an elderly gentleman in the clubhouse had lent me his.

So I did what made sense to me. I kissed the putter that won it for me.

Some day, who knows? Maybe I'll kiss it again as I slip on the green jacket after the Masters.

# THE GREAT JIMMY D.

Any time I spent with Jimmy Demaret is a special memory, but the really unforgettable moment was that day we were being introduced on television before we teed off in a charity benefit at the Los Angeles Open.

Thousands of people surrounded the first tee. The tournament officials had come up with a great idea – pairing past LA Open champions like Jimmy with current players like me. Jimmy, the original technicolor player on the tour, looked great – wearing all those bright colours and with his white hair. As usual, he had a big smile on his face. Hell, they didn't call him Sunny Jimmy Demaret for nothing!

The announcer turned to me and asked, 'Lee, how does it feel to be playing with this great legend, Jimmy Demaret?'

I thought I should try to be funny. 'It just feels fantastic,' I said, 'but he's old enough to be my father.'

'And she was a good old gal!' Jimmy said, never changing expression.

For the next 18 holes, I kept my mouth shut.

Jimmy was probably the funniest man I've ever been around. Everything was so natural with him, just part of his great personality.

He had a world of friends, including a bunch of old show-business stars who loved golf. Phil Harris told me he picked up a lot of lines from Jimmy and that Bing Crosby did, too. Back in the sixties when Gay Brewer became a big name in golf, Phil Harris got a lot of publicity when he cracked, 'Gay Brewer ... that sounds like a fag winemaker from Modesto!' Jimmy had said it first. Same thing with that description of Sam Snead's putting style at the Legends of Golf: 'It looks like he's basting a turkey.'

Everything Jimmy said was original, just like his life in golf.

After Jimmy played a round at Champions Golf Club – a beautiful place near Houston, which he owned with Jack Burke – he loved to strip down to his underwear in the locker room, stand at the bar with a glass of red wine, and tell stories.

He remembered all those wonderful times back in the thirties when golf pros bounced around the country, making a buck any way they could. Those were the days when Walter Hagen was a living legend and young players from Texas like Ben Hogan, Byron Nelson, and Jimmy were just happy to be living and playing golf. They had no idea that some day they'd be legends, too.

The tour always started in California so Jimmy left Houston as a rookie in 1935, eager to give it a shot. He had his clubs, a car, and $600 he had borrowed from Sam Maceo, who ran a nightclub in Galveston, from an oilman named D. B. McDaniel, and from Ben Bernie, a bandleader. The only problem was he couldn't reach California without driving through El Paso, which is right by Juárez.

Naturally, Jimmy found himself taking a left turn into Mexico for a look. And, of course, he made friends quickly. Next thing he knew a man asked him if he wanted to shoot some pool.

'We played three days,' Jimmy said. 'I lost the car the first day, the clubs the second, and the six hundred dollars the third. So I sent the pawn ticket for my clubs to my brother Milton and asked him to get them out of hock and have them shipped to me in California. Then I boarded my train – a freight.'

Now I can appreciate his experience. When I lived in El Paso I spent some nights at Juárez Racetrack after which they had to send me back across the border C.O.D.

Once Jimmy reached California he had to live on sandwiches and cheap wine for a couple of weeks, and then his game saved him. He won a few hundred dollars and he was on his way, throwing parties and wearing those fantastic clothes.

Jimmy played in pink shoes and polka-dot slacks. He wore lavender, gold, orange, red, aqua, emerald, and maroon as naturally as all the other players wore their basic black and white. He ordered ladies' pastel fabrics from abroad and had his tailor cut his slacks, shirts, and coats from them. Then he had matching shoes made. Hell, he had more than five hundred hats.

The LA Open always attracted a lot of stars – and starlets.

'We knew everybody in Hollywood,' Jimmy said. 'It was pretty impressive to be hanging around Bing Crosby and folks like that all the

time. And there were an awful lot of dandy little old gals around. We didn't know who they were. They had different names then. But we later realized that they were people like Susan Hayward.'

Jimmy told us about Lloyd Mangrum, who was a sharp cardplayer, arriving in New Orleans on the eve of Mardi Gras. The town was packed, and Mangrum was so broke he gladly took two days of free room and board at the city jail. And he told about one night in Florida when Walter Hagen and Joe Kirkwood walked into the Biltmore Hotel after fishing in the Everglades and dumped everything they caught in the lobby, including a small alligator.

Wherever Jimmy was, there was laughter. Once during a rain delay at the Colonial Tournament in Fort Worth, the players got up a pool on the outcome. Jimmy patted Roberto de Vicenzo on the back and said, 'Roberto, please play as good as you can. I'm betting on you to be low Mexican.'

And there was the time Jimmy was invited to New York to be the mystery guest on 'What's My Line?' – the popular television quiz show of the 1950s where masked panelists tried to guess a celebrity's identity.

He was asked to use a back elevator to reach the NBC studios so he wouldn't be recognized. Well, Jimmy spent the afternoon at Toots Shor's bar, and when he rushed into the NBC buiilding, he forgot and took the wrong elevator.

When Jimmy's turn on the show came, the first panelist immediately asked if he was Jimmy Demaret. Everybody was shocked. John Daly, the moderator, asked the man how he knew it was Demaret. He said it was easy. On the elevator before the show, some stranger with a big smile had stuck out his hand and said, 'Hi! I'm Jimmy Demaret!'

For all of his fun, Jimmy also was a tremendous player.

A few years ago I invited Gary Player's son, Wayne, to spend some time with me at the Houston Open while his father took Wayne's little sister, Amanda, to Florida to visit Walt Disney World. As soon as we arrived, I took Wayne to Champions to play.

Wayne was sixteen at the time and I asked him, 'Have you ever met Mr Demaret?' He said, 'No, but my father has spoken highly of him.' When we reached the 6th tee, there came a golf cart with Jimmy in it. He introduced himself to Wayne, whose eyes got as big as silver dollars, and we invited him to play a few holes with us.

Jimmy was almost seventy then, but he stood up there cold and just shanked the driver down the fairway, and then he shanked the 3-wood on the green and he made the putt for a 3. I made a 5 for a bogey, and Wayne did, too.

The 7th hole was Jimmy's favourite, a dogleg right. Jimmy faded it down the fairway, faded a 4-iron on the green, and made the putt for another birdie. I parred and Wayne bogeyed. Then he asked me, 'How good was this guy before?'

The last time I saw Jimmy was in the spring of 1983 at the Legends of Golf, which he helped create and which helped make senior golf so popular in the US. I was there doing TV commentary for NBC; Jimmy dropped by the booth and visited during the show. Jack Fleck came up the fairway, and I mentioned he was most famous for beating Ben Hogan in an 18-hole play-off for the US Open title in 1955.

'Yeah,' Jimmy said, 'that was like catching lightning in a fruit jar.'

I thought of that when I heard the news of Jimmy's death a few months later. It was a couple of days after Christmas. Jimmy died suddenly at Champions.

Having Jimmy Demaret in this world, with his wonderful personality and laughter and style, was like catching lightning in a fruit jar. I wish I could have bottled his laughter to take on down days.

# FUZZY

Golf needs Fuzzy Zoeller. He has a big game and a great spirit that gives everyone a lift. He makes you feel better about what you're doing.

There's nobody I would rather be around at a tournament than Fuzzy. I wish we could inject some of his personality into every new player who joins the tour. It would be a lot livelier out there, and the quality of the golf would improve, too.

A classic example of Fuzzy's wonderful temperament was the trick he pulled when he was leading the New Orleans tournament. Everybody was on the putting green, so Fuzzy got a chair, sat at the end of the green, and lit a cigarette. He sat there smoking and drinking a Coke while he watched everyone putt.

'I don't need to be practising,' he said real loud. 'I'm leading this tournament. You guys go on and practise, because you're behind.'

He didn't win the tournament, but that's the way Fuzzy is. He's just a funny man. And he can be just as funny when he thinks he's losing. It was terrific how he stood in the 18th fairway waving his white towel in surrender after watching Greg Norman sink that incredible long putt in the final round of the 1984 US Open. Fuzzy thought Greg had made a 3 and Fuzzy was grinning and conceding the championship. Actually, it gave Greg a 4 and forced a play-off – which Fuzzy won; but his first reaction was pure and refreshing.

Fuzzy also won the Masters in 1979, so winning the 1984 US Open championship gave him two majors, taking away any pressure he may have felt about proving he's a top-class player. But his back trouble, which began with a high school basketball injury, flared up again. He finally had to withdraw for the rest of the year and have surgery. He had two discs removed, and that left a question mark hanging over his future.

I can feel for him because I've had a back surgery twice; it was a

tremendous struggle to get in condition to play again. But I believe he still can have a good career if he doesn't push himself too fast. And for God's sake, Fuzzy, don't practise too much. Believe me, you can win without it.

And he did. In March of 1985, less than a month after rejoining the tour, Fuzzy proved himself by winning the Bay Hill Classic – smiling all the way. We need Fuzzy. Besides, I like to hear his needling.

If you hit a bad shot, Fuzzy will say, 'Geez, you're swinging awful at that thing!'

If you miss a putt five inches to the right, he'll come over and say, 'Damn, I could have sworn you made that one. You put such a great stroke on it.'

If some guy who never said anything like that before suddenly blurted that out, you'd nail him with your putter right there on the green. But you can't get mad at Fuzzy – he's like that all the time.

He and I once were in a field of ten players at a match called the Colonial Shoot-out in Forth Worth, where one player would be eliminated on each hole on the back 9. When we teed off on no. 10, I hit a wood and everyone else hit an iron. Fuzzy couldn't let that pass.

'Hey, Lee, put on a skirt and go on up to the front tees,' he yelled. The gallery roared. I loved it.

# ZORRO AND MISTER X

If you want to talk about ageing gracefully, let me tell you about Don January and Miller Barber. They had long, successful careers on the regular tour and then when they turned fifty they just floated into that happy hunting ground – the seniors tour.

They've been the hottest players out there for several years, battling for the money championship. I believe both of them can play in those seniors tournaments as long as they want to because of how they play and how they feel about the game.

Don is the classic flat-belly, tall and lanky and never seems in a hurry to do anything. Miller is anything but. He's shorter, heavier, and still likes to wear those sunglasses that helped him get the nickname Mister X, years ago.

I have a very early memory of Don: I was a kid in North Dallas, caddying at the old DAC Country Club, when he played there occasionally. He was a star college player then for North Texas State, and his teams won several national championships. I remember he'd come out there with his collar turned up to keep the sun off his neck, wearing black pants, black shirt, black socks, and black shoes. All he needed was the Lone Ranger's mask and he could be Zorro.

He was a hero as far as I was concerned. Being Mexican, black is one of my favourite colours. Maybe it's because we can wear it for a long time without noticing the dirt.

Don was the first player I knew who went on the pro golf tour. The first tournament he ever won was the Dallas Open at Preston Hollow in 1956. I listened to it on the radio and thought it was great that a local boy won.

It's been a long journey from then to now. Don has shown a talent for playing good golf at any age.

He won the PGA Championship in 1967, the year I started on the tour, then did some golf-course construction in Dallas. He and Billy Martindale put together Royal Oaks, where I am a member, and it was a tremendous design. I don't think there's another golf course in Dallas as tough as Royal Oaks.

Don proved just how good his game really is in 1975. He came back on the tour at the age of forty-five after working two years full time in golf-course design. The recession had hit the construction business hard, so he just strolled back out there, won the Texas Open at San Antonio, and earned more money that year than ever before – $69,000. The next year, 1976, he won the Tournament of Champions and increased his annual earnings to almost $95,000.

When the seniors tour started to come alive, Don was ready to gear down on the regular tour and wait for his fiftieth birthday. In 1979 he came out and played our tour to kind of 'warm up' for the seniors, and he won almost $80,000. After that, nobody was surprised by how great he's been as a senior. He's stringy, he still hits the ball a long way, and he putts fairly good. He doesn't putt as well as Billy Casper, but he's in a helluva lot better shape.

When Miller Barber turned fifty in 1981, senior golf got a really good rivalry. He and Don are old friends, but Don said he decided he had to change one thing.

'For years Miller and I played a practice round together on Tuesday before the tournament,' Don said. 'We usually played against Ben Crenshaw and Bruce Lietzke, and while we were out there I would give Miller a golf lesson. Miller looked forward to that, and he played pretty well. But when he turned fifty and we started battling each other in the seniors tournaments, I told Miller, "I'm not ever giving you another lesson." '

Miller is such a good-natured guy that someone is always needling him a little. In his way, he can use that needle, too. When Miller was asked to make the opening remarks at a dinner before a major tournament, he looked at the other pros at the head table and shrugged. 'Here I am,' he said. 'First again.' If golf were like rodeos, with the top competitors going out three or four times a week, Miller would be one of them. He says he plays so many tournaments because he loves the money, but I know better: he'd play for nothing if he had to.

After Don overtook Miller in one tournament, I said, 'Don, you seem to have Miller's number, don't you?' Don grinned. 'Mex,' he said, 'if Miller Barber gets to playing too good, I just take a cattle prod, touch him on the side, and give him a little shock. That takes care of him for the day.'

Miller may just shake his head when he hears that kind of stuff, waiting for the chance to get back with a funny line.

In 1983 we were partners in the Jeremy Ranch Tournament, which pairs seniors and juniors. We didn't start too well, but in the late rounds we were hot. All the way through the course, Miller kept studying the leader board. I figured he wanted to see how close we were getting to Bob Goalby and Mike Reid, who were leading the tournament.

At the 16th tee, he looked at the scores again and told me, 'All I'm interested in is tying or beating Don January.' Well, we shot 59 the last round, so Miller got his wish.

He got the nickname Mister X back in his early days on the tour, when he was out there nearly every week making money but not getting much media attention. Miller was a bachelor then and he kept quiet about his social life, but it was less of a mystery than he meant it to be as the other players would frequently find him – even in the most secluded nightspots – with yet another good-looking woman.

Just before he turned fifty, Miller gave himself another nickname. Some of us were on the practice tee and we asked him how he felt he would do playing against the seniors.

'Mmm, mmm, mmm,' he said. 'You can't believe what I'm going to do on the seniors tour. Man, I'm going to feel like Jesse James, just robbing everybody.'

Then, the first tournament he played in, Miller didn't win. Doug Ford did. When we heard that, we figured we should send him a telegram saying, 'Doug Ford shot Jesse James.'

Miller may never live that down but it didn't slow him down. Like the rodeo cowboy, he just found some more action.

# THE ONE AND ONLY

Anyone who hung out at Tenison Park in the early 1960s soon knew about Titanic Thompson. He was a legendary hustler and gambler, a man who might show up anywhere that people enjoyed games with money on the line.

So in the summer of 1966, a few months after I went to work as the pro and club handyman at Horizon Hills, I wasn't surprised to see Ti appear in El Paso.

I'll never forget that morning when he stepped out of his taxi in front of the clubhouse. As Ti squinted his eyes in the desert sun he looked like an ageing Clint Eastwood. Clint made a movie called *A Fistful of Dollars*. That title pretty well fitted Ti's line of work, too. I'm sure he had heard at Tenison Park about those cotton farmers at Horizon Hills who loved to bet big money. He came to El Paso to check them out.

Ti was tall and slim, an easygoing type with an ol' Texas drawl. He fitted in with the atmosphere at Horizon Hills real well and immediately joined the club. But after a week he had robbed our members of so much money at everything – pitching at the line, blackjack, poker, playing golf right- and left-handed – that they asked him real nice if he would leave.

Man, that was one busy week!

We even had a call from the Texas Rangers, saying they knew Titanic Thompson was at the club and that we had poker games and other gambling going all night long. Under Texas law then any place that sold liquor had to close at midnight, but even if we cut the liquor off we still had guys there until eight o'clock in the morning. The Rangers told us to stop it or they would have to shut us down.

If you saw Ti once, you'd always remember him. He had the youngest pair of hands and clearest blue eyes I ever saw. He was probably close to seventy years old then but his long, slender hands looked like they belonged to someone twenty-three, twenty-four years old. And his eyes were also young. Maybe it was because he never exposed them to much sun.

I never saw Ti drive a car. He always came out to the club in a taxi and he left in a taxi. I never saw him take a drink and I never saw him smoke. His reflexes were better than most guys' and he could see what was going on. He did everything possible to ensure himself of having the edge in anything he bet on, and he wanted to be sure he went into anything at least even.

One night during a poker game Ti was looking at his cards and one club member was speaking Spanish. Ti put his cards down and said, 'Gentlemen, I want to tell you now before this gets out of hand. We're speaking only English in the room.' He didn't know if this fellow was looking at his hand or somebody else's. There were a lot of people lined up around the walls, and Ti wasn't going to risk being at a disadvantage.

He didn't play that much golf in his older days, but he did get out on the course at Horizon Hills. One day he was playing a guy for a little money, and I went out and joined them on the 9th hole. Ti was playing left-handed and he said, 'C'mon, pro, you want to play this hole?'

'Yeah,' I said, 'But I don't have any clubs.'

'There's mine,' Ti said, nodding at his left-handed clubs.

'What do you want to bet?' I asked.

'I'll bet you five dollars on this hole,' Ti told me. It was a par-4, water on the right. So I hit his 3-wood left-handed. I hit his 5-iron on the green, 2-putted for a par, and I beat him.

'Here's your five dollars,' Ti said. 'You're a goddamn freak.'

Ti never beat me out of a nickel, because I wouldn't play any of his games. I used his clubs and beat him playing my game, which I had had a little experience with left-handed.

He liked my style. One morning he got me off in a corner at breakfast and offered me a deal as his partner.

'Forget the PGA Tour,' he told me. 'There's no money in it.' I believe Ti was thinking about the thirties, forties, and early fifties and how hard it was to make a living out there then. I don't think he could comprehend what was happening with the tour, how commercial it was becoming, and how much money a good golfer could make.

He said, 'Why don't you just travel the country with me? You play golf

and I'll do the betting.' It sounded very inviting, but I had this dream of going on the tour and becoming one of the world's top players.

There are so many stories about Ti that I don't know how true they are. Some things may have been exaggerated, but I know he led a fantastic life. He figured everything has a trick to it. The best tale I ever heard was about Ti beating a guy out of $5000 in New York back in the thirties. He took a top hat, set it upside down on the floor in a sitting room in a hotel suite, then stepped in the connecting room and closed the door with about an inch clearance above the floor. He then bet the guy $5000 he could take a deck of cards and put a dozen of the fifty-two cards into the top hat by flipping them under the door.

Ti put seventeen in there and the guy never knew how he did it. Ti had a friend in the next room who went out on the fire escape, slipped into the sitting room, grabbed the cards as they came under the door, and put them in the hat. After the first seventeen he went back out on the fire escape, closed the window, and returned to his room. There was enough time because Ti still had to flip thirty-five more cards under the door.

He made a fortune with little things like that.

You often see highway mileage signs like DALLAS 17 MILES. Well, Ti would dig the sign up and move it 5 miles out and then bet people about the distance. He might not do it then. He might wait five years. Then one day he would drive by with some guy and say, 'Hey, what does that sign say?'

'Seventeen miles.'

'Hey, I'll bet you it's closer to twenty.'

That's all he did. Ti figured there was a fool born every day, and he dreamed up things like that to make money off them.

Sometimes it didn't work, of course. I saw Arnold Salinas beat him out of $50 in the Horizon Hills clubhouse.

With the exception of Bob Rosburg, Ti was the best I've ever seen at flipping a card and making it sail through the air. It's an art and I can't do it. I flip them and the cards go straight down. But Ti could stand 15 feet from a sliced water-melon, flip cards, and they would stick in the melon. Well, once Arnold was trying to flip a card over the cigarette machine and couldn't do it, when Ti walked by. 'Tell you what I'm going to do, cowboy,' Ti told him. 'I'm going to bet you fifty dollars you can't flip a card over that cigarette machine.'

Arnold held up the card. 'This card?' he asked.

'Yeah,' Ti said.

So Arnold took the card, wadded it into a little ball, and flipped it over the machine.

'You run into one of these guys every once in a while,' Ti said.

Ti had a trick to making long putts. He would take a water hose, leave it on a green that had just been watered, and then move it the next day. Then they mowed the green and that left a trough. You could putt a ball and it would roll right down the trough into the hole. I saw Ti bet a guy he could sink 3 out of 5 putts from 30 feet, then send the ball right through that trough.

Everything he did he had researched and he knew the odds. He knew he could do it before he did it. Besides being a great poker and blackjack player, he made it his business to know all this: he would bet that if he dealt five cards and turned them over there would be a pair in those five cards. Ti had studied the odds.

I'm sure he sometimes ran into a guy who could beat him pitching at the line, but Ti had a good gambler's sense. He'd take his loss and get out instead of doubling up, doing something stupid trying to get even.

I asked him how he got the name Titanic, and his answer didn't make sense. He said he was in a bar once, bet a guy he could jump the pool table flat-footed, and when he did it the guy said, 'You sank me like the *Titanic*.'

I've also heard he got the nickname because he got off the *Titanic* before it sank. As I understand the history of the *Titanic*, very few men got off – mostly women and children. I heard he dressed like a woman and got into a lifeboat, but I have no idea how true that is. Maybe somewhere along the line he *told* somebody he got off the *Titanic* and the story grew from there. Or maybe they called him Titanic simply because he drowned everybody.

Ti died a few years ago, and he spent his last days in a rest home. Again, I don't know how true it is, but I heard that when Ti died he owned every wheelchair, every crutch, and every walking cane there and leased them back for a dime or quarter a week to the man who operated the home. He had won them playing checkers with the old people there.

He was beautiful.

# THE MAN WITH EVERYTHING

Years ago I played with Ramon Sota of Spain in the World Cup and in a couple of tournaments in Mexico, and he told me he had a nephew who was a tremendous golfer. I paid no attention to him. Everywhere I go I hear someone say, 'Oh, I've got a good one coming up.'

But Uncle Ramon was right. His nephew is Seve Ballesteros.

The first time I saw Seve play was in the 1976 British Open at Royal Birkdale. I was having a lot of back trouble, so I withdrew from the tournament and just watched. I remember Seve and Johnny Miller playing the last round together, Miller eventually winning the championship and Seve finishing second. I couldn't believe a kid nineteen years old knew exactly what he was doing with that golf ball. He had so many shots they could have called him the Spanish Armada.

I met Seve for the first time a little later at a tournament in Europe and we hit it off right away. Maybe it's because we both caddied as kids or maybe it's because Seve likes how I can talk to him in Spanish. We've always been good friends. He can probably do more with a golf ball than I can, but, hell, that's no disgrace. It's amazing. He's got every shot in the book.

We always evaluate a player by what the Lord gave him. In Seve's case, the Lord gave him the good looks, the body, the strength, the good putting stroke, the good bunker play, the good wedge game and length. He can hit a 1-iron as far as I can hit a driver.

The Lord also gave him a temper. Seve gets a little mad at himself when he misses a shot. He just doesn't believe that it's supposed to happen. And he can get equally mad at somebody else. The perfect example was how he behaved at the 1980 US Open at Baltusrol. He was disqualified for missing his tee time in the second round, and he stormed

off, saying he would never play in the US Open again. Oh, I did a lot of those things myself once. I stuck my foot in my mouth and I suffered for it. If I'd never said anything about the Masters I probably would have won it years ago. But as Seve grows older he'll learn to control his emotions. Other than that, he has everything going for him.

He already has won all over the world. By the time he was twenty-seven he had won the Masters and the British Open twice and had been very successful in his limited appearances in other US tournaments.

In 1983, Seve announced he was going to spend some time on the US tour and some people sneered. 'Well, bring him over here,' they said. 'We'll show him how to play.' They didn't think he would hold up under all the demands and strong competition on the US tour. Well, Seve played eight tournaments, won two of them, and finished in the top five in two others. He earned $210,000 and then went home to Spain.

After that, I told people, 'If you look at what he won compared to how many tournaments he played, you should tell him to stay home and not come over here and play.' I don't think anyone in America will doubt Seve's ability again.

It seems like every decade there comes a player who's outstanding and stands apart from everyone else. Seve is one of them. I don't think he has scratched the surface yet in showing his full ability. I think he's a helluva lot better player than the world has seen so far.

He comes from a great family, one that really helped him learn to play golf. His older brother Manuel has played a lot as a pro, and his other brothers know the game, too. Their father was a farmer and their home was next to a golf course, so they all played a lot as boys. But Seve was the one who came out on top in world-class competition simply because his brother taught him everything he knew. He was able to absorb and execute everything his brother wanted him to do.

A lot of times a teacher can't execute the shot he wants you to hit, but he can tell you how to do it. Some people adapt much quicker than others, and that's what Seve did.

If Seve is going to play in the United States on a regular basis, I think the best thing for him is to get married. I know that sounds like, 'Hey, you're trying to slow him down.' But I'm sincere about this. Married, he would have a companion, someone he loved very much, to travel with. That would keep him from getting homesick; you can adapt to just about anyplace if you're with the person you love.

Seve is a good friend and I wish him well. When his book, *The Young*

*Champion*, was published, I was honoured that he asked me to write the introduction to it. Years from now he may do a second book, *The Old Champion*. I'll be pleased to write the introduction to that one too.

# CHI CHI

Pound for pound, Chi Chi Rodriguez has to be the greatest golfer in the world. He's also one of the funniest and certainly the kindest.

Chi Chi always wants to say something nice about somebody. One time he and I were paired with two players from the women's tour in an exhibition. When we finished, there was none of this kiss-on-the-cheek business. We just shook hands and they started striding off toward the clubhouse. Chi Chi watched them admiringly for a moment.

'There,' he said, 'go two perfect gentlemen.'

Like me, Chi Chi got hooked on golf early in life and has always loved the game. 'Golf is the most fun you can have,' he said, 'without taking off your clothes' – an old joke, I know, but I can't argue with the sentiment.

Chi Chi was the first player on the professional golf tour who really grabbed my attention. This was back in 1963 and 1964, when I was playing a lot of golf at Tenison Park in Dallas and working at Hardy's Driving Range. I knew something about those great old Texas golfers like Ben Hogan, Byron Nelson, and Jimmy Demaret, but the only other thing I knew was that Arnold Palmer and Jack Nicklaus were the new superstars. It wasn't until I started playing the tour a few years later that I realized Bobby Jones wasn't Robert Trent Jones, the golf-course designer.

When I heard about this little guy named Juan Rodriguez who was out-driving Nicklaus and Palmer and winning some tournaments, I thought, 'Hey, that Mexican must be something else!' Then I heard he was a Puerto Rican, which was fine. I knew with a name like Juan Rodriguez he damn sure wasn't Irish.

They said he was a dynamic fellow who had a lot of colour and really put on a show when he played. He liked to dance around the greens and play swordsman with his putter. Chi Chi always wears a little straw hat. When he made a putt he would put his hat over the hole, then get on

his knees and peek under his hat to see if his ball still was in the cup. The gallery loved it. Chi Chi was different, and he could play with the best of them.

When I joined the tour in 1967, I met Chi Chi. What I saw was a guy about my height (5 feet, 7 inches) but a lot thinner. Chi Chi never has weighed more than about 130 pounds, but he hits the ball with tremendous power. I got to know him as a person and a human being and found there was much more to him than his wisecracks and funny tricks.

I did a couple of exhibitions with Chi Chi for the Heart Association in San Juan, and I was amazed at how the people of Puerto Rico love this man. But people everywhere love him. He's fun to be around, he's generous, and he never has forgotten where he came from.

As a boy in Puerto Rico, he wanted to play golf but had no money to buy clubs and balls. So Chi Chi hit tin cans with limbs from a guava tree. He started caddying, but when he was nineteen he joined the army because he could make more money to help at home. Chi Chi came from a large family and he always shared whatever he had with them.

And he shares with so many. I never see him that he doesn't ask, 'Do you need anything?' He loves kids. On tour I've seen him take a bunch of kids and buy them tickets, hot dogs, and drinks.

The bottom line on Chi Chi is this: if everybody in this world were like him you wouldn't need borders or passports. Everyone would feel at home everywhere. And you sure wouldn't need any jailers.

A lot of people say that I'm a lot like him, but I'm really not. I know I'll never be a match for Chi Chi Rodriguez.

# MOPPING UP

For years I was remembered at the Masters for all the wrong reasons. Twice, in 1970 and 1971, I refused my invitation to play there after loudly criticizing the layout at Augusta National because it has no rough to penalize guys who hit it crooked, and the hills are in places that favour the long knockers.

Then I came back and immediately got hot about a mix-up over a ticket for my caddy during my first practice round. I was close to packing up and leaving again before Clifford Roberts, the man who founded the Masters with Bobby Jones, explained that the season ticket I had bought for my caddy wasn't good on practice days; he needed a separate ticket for those. It's not that way at any other golf tournament in the world, but that's the Masters for you. They do things their own way.

That's why I felt proud that I finally could be remembered at Augusta for doing something right. On that rainy Saturday in April 1984 I won one from the Masters brass because I stood firm for what I knew was right – standing ankle deep in water at the time.

Part of the Masters tradition is all those names they give to different holes and bridges and ponds and flower beds on the course. I don't know what the 16th green is called, but since that day I've felt it should be known as the Mexican Standoff.

You know the definition of a Mexican standoff: we lost our ass but we got out alive. That's what happened to the Masters brass there.

When George Archer, David Graham and I reached the 16th green, we shouldn't have been putting, because the greens were too wet. My ball was about 20 feet from the cup, and so was Graham's. Archer's was about 30 feet away, and the entire hole was covered with water.

I know what the Masters people were thinking. We were on national television and they were insisting we finish this round so we could finish the tournament on time Sunday. There was an official on the green and I asked him, 'What are we going to do about putting?'

'Well, you have to putt,' he said.

'What do you mean I *have* to putt?' I asked.

'We've been given instructions to keep play moving,' he told me.

'You can't putt to that cup,' I told him. 'It's surrounded by water.'

'Well, I can't help it,' he said. 'Everybody else has been putting.'

So George Archer went ahead and 3-putted. The official looked at me and I just stood there.

'If you think I'm going to putt, you better call the clubhouse and get your lunch,' I said. 'We're going to be out here awhile.'

He got on the radio with tournament headquarters and said, 'Trevino won't putt.'

'Yeah,' I said, 'and tell them why I won't putt.'

He listened to their answer and nodded. 'They say you're going to have to putt,' he said.

'No, I'm not,' I said. 'The rules state that if you are on the putting surface and cannot move your ball to a dry surface to putt, the green has to be towelled or squeegeed. Play has to be suspended until it is.'

'Well, they say you have to putt,' he said. The guy sounded like a recording.

'Then you had better call somebody else,' I said.

He called Clyde Mangum, the deputy commissioner of the PGA Tour, and told him, 'Trevino won't putt on the sixteenth.'

'Why not?' Mangum asked.

'The hole is surrounded by water,' the official told him.

And Mangum shot right back: 'He doesn't have to putt. You are going to have to towel or squeegee that green.' And that was that.

When all the squeegees came out, I got a standing ovation from about fifteen thousand people around the 16th green. The officials there knew the rule. It was just that they were told to keep play moving and nobody was going to mess around and delay that golf tournament. Again, they were dictating their own rules.

After they finally did the the right thing, I wanted to show the television audience how deep the water was on the course. So when I went to 17 I skipped along and dragged my club behind me. Water churned in my wake as if an outboard motorboat had just come through.

Better yet, I should have tried a jackknife dive before swimming down the middle of the fairway. But I made my point. And I had one more memorable Masters. Maybe if I hadn't decided the wide-open Augusta course wasn't for my game I would have won it by now.

# WORLD OF WORDS

It had been a rare day for me at the Masters. I shot a 68 in the first round and felt in a talkative mood when I sat down at the platform in the press interview room.

Maybe too talkative.

This was in 1984, and I had just been married a few months to Claudia Bove. The media had started calling her Claudia II; they were fascinated that my new wife had the same name as my old one.

'You've got another Claudia,' one writer said. 'Any reason for that?'

'Yeah,' I said. 'I didn't have to change the initials on the towels or the sheets.'

That got heavy play in the press, and even though she didn't say anything we both knew there was another side to it. When my last marriage broke up I had no towels left – initialled or otherwise. It was time to stop reaching for a laugh and to retire that line.

Something happens to me at press conferences. There's a chemistry about those things that gets me going. The questions, the give-and-the-take stimulate me much more than if I just stood on a stage and started talking.

After my first US Open victory in 1968, somebody asked me how I was going to spend the prize money of $30,000.

'I may buy the Alamo,' I said, 'and give it back to Mexico.'

Hey, people still remember that back in Texas, as they did when I went to San Antonio a few weeks later for the PGA Championship. Everyone kept mentioning the Alamo, so I took a tour of it. When I came outside, I said, 'Well, I'm not gonna buy this place. It doesn't have indoor plumbing.'

At press conferences I don't know exactly what I will be asked, so how can I know exactly what I am going to say? At one US Open I was talking about the weird round I had played. 'A few times out there,' I said, 'I thought I was losing my mind.'

A guy in the back row smirked when I said that. 'Maybe you need a psychiatrist,' he said.

'Yeah,' I said, 'how about yours?'

I've enjoyed a great deal of media coverage around the world. Because I've had some success and some strange things have happened to me in my golf career, people seem interested in what I've done and what I'm thinking. But sometimes I'm a little surprised to read 'the latest from Trevino.'

Greg Norman, the big hitter from Australia who's known as the Great White Shark, was a sensation at the 1984 US Open. He made some incredible shots to force Fuzzy Zoeller into a play-off. Everybody who wrote about him touched on his nickname, which he got because he likes to shoot sharks while fishing off the Australian coast.

Some of those stories had me saying, 'I don't mind playing golf with him, but I'll be damned if I'll go swimming with him.' That may be funny, but I don't know how it got started. I didn't say it.

That remark was harmless, so it's no big deal. But some comments I supposedly have said have not been.

One of the most embarrassing lines I ever was quoted as saying appeared in the Chicago papers during the Western Open. Larry Ziegler and I went into the tournament office to pick up some badges, and Larry made a crack about Hubert Green.

'Hubert Green,' he said, 'was so ugly when he was a baby that his mother tied a porkchop around his neck to get the dog to play with him.'

The next day that was in the paper as a quote from me. I don't know why. I wouldn't say that about anybody. And Hubert Green happens to be a damn good friend of mine. I guess a sportswriter had come in the office later and someone had repeated that crack. That someone remembered I had been there at the time and somehow wound up giving me 'credit' for it. If the writer had to use it at all, I wish to hell he had gotten the source right.

But in a mass interview with hundreds of writers I can understand why those without tape recorders confuse some things I say. The mouth is faster than the hand. I talk a hundred miles an hour, and there's no way someone can write down everything I say. Now there's no problem interviewing Lyn Lott. He's an easygoing guy from Georgia and he says one word about every four seconds. You don't even have to shorthand him. You can get everything he says in longhand.

But it bothers me when I come across a writer who's been drinking all day and is asking me questions just to hear himself talk.

A guy did that to me at Memphis once. He must have asked me seven or eight questions and I kept answering them. Finally I said, 'Sir, you must have a helluva memory.'

'Why is that?' he asked me.

'The only damn thing you have in your hand is a beer,' I told him. 'You haven't written down a word I've said.'

He left right after that. I guess he needed another beer.

# SHOTS — SOME HOT AND SOME NOT

I've seen enough crazy shots to know they happen in the best of families. On my first trip to the World Series of Golf at Firestone in 1968 I saw Gary Player go for the pin and see his ball almost wind up in a lady's blouse.

It was a beautiful golf shot, too. Gary just hit too much club. It was the 12th hole, a par-3, and the pin was tucked back right. Gary hit a 5-iron right at the hole, and the ball landed on the back of the green and hit this lady in the chest.

Luckily she had her arms crossed and the ball came right down on her arms and breast. She was really embarrassed. Gary got to drop the ball, naturally, and he made a 3. The crazy coincidence was that the lady turned out to be the wife of Mark McCormack, Gary's manager, the sports entrepreneur.

Weird things happen out there. Once in Cleveland I saw a dog pick a ball up off the green and run off with it! I've even seen a ball land in a cup of beer. A guy ducked, put his hands up, and the ball dropped neatly in his beer. Once we hollered 'Fore!' when a guy sliced his drive, and the ball wound up in a man's hip pocket. The ball went in so fine the man never knew it.

Of course, people tend to save a lot of shots for you if you have a big gallery. I won my first Memphis Open that way in 1971.

They wanted me to win so bad that they wouldn't move. If I hit a ball that looked like it was going over the green, I always hollered 'Fore!' but the crowd frequently would kick at it, moving it closer to the green. I'm not the only player who's been helped that way. A lot of people have won tournaments because of supporting fans.

Strange shots? Well, a lot of times you get up next to a bunker that's real deep and you can't stand in the bunker because the ball is up to your chin. So I face the opposite direction and hit it backward. I've made par doing that. You'd be surprised how easy it is to hit.

I hit an unusual shot at Augusta one year, but it wasn't in the tournament. I bet a guy I could skip the ball five times across the lake on 16 and knock it on the green. I took a 1-iron and skipped it about six times. It skipped through the water up onto the bank, and I 2-putted for a par.

And once at Pensacola I was so deep in the trees I couldn't see the green. I actually had to shoot about 60 yards away from the green to the right. I took a sand wedge and duck-hooked the ball around the trees. It stopped about 20 feet from the hole.

Sometimes it seems the ball simply is destined to go in the hole. A big reason I repeated as British Open champion in 1972 was a totally unexpected chip-in I made on the 17th while playing with Tony Jacklin: but my chili was so hot at that moment I couldn't appreciate it.

That was strictly a give-up shot. I was so damn mad because I had just chipped the ball over the green and onto the hill. When I walked over there my anger was making me see stars. I had blown the tournament and I knew it.

I took the 9-iron out and chopped on the ball – and it went in from around 20 feet. No excitement. I just walked over and sat on my bag. I hadn't gotten over being mad, and I really didn't give a damn whether it went in or not. Usually when I chip in I dance around and jump in the air and go crazy. This time, nothing. It never registered on me what it meant until Jacklin missed a little putt of 2½ feet.

I once made a difficult chip because I had to hit it in tall grass going straight downhill. You could stand there with $10 now and I probably couldn't get it up or down or even come close.

Then a few years later in the Benson & Hedges in York, I went into the last round, and Seve Ballesteros had me by 5 shots; I was in third place. On the 4th hole I hit a driver, then I took a 1-iron and hit a beautiful shot. The ball went 206 yards into the hole for a 2.

And then Seve did something totally unexpected. He knocked it out of bounds and wound up making a 7. I went on to win the tournament, beating Neil Coles in a play-off. Seve finished 1 shot behind us, tied for third.

When I won the Tournament Players Championship at Sawgrass in 1980, some people raved that I made a fabulous shot on the 18th, the last round. I didn't agree.

That's a par-5 and I had a 1-shot lead over Ben Crenshaw when I hit a little wedge 100 yards over a bunker. Nobody was stopping his ball on the green, and I hit it low because I really wanted to pinch that thing. It went up, took two hops, and everyone thought it was going over. Then it went *zssspt!* and kind of curled and came back to the hole. It stopped about 8 feet from the cup, so that was it.

It looks great to people but I expect to do that. That's what years of training and practice are supposed to do for you. If you *don't* hit some of those shots you're not going to win.

Maybe the greatest shot was my drive at number 17 on the last round when I won the 1974 PGA at Tanglewood. I had a 2-shot lead over Jack Nicklaus, but this was a very difficult hole – a sharp dogleg left.

I decided to hook it, which is something I've never been famous for, and it came off perfect. I hooked it around that corner, and Nicklaus looked at me as though I had just lost my mind.

Hell, I was surprised, too. I've never been able to draw the ball too well. I lose too many to the left, and a lot of times I leave too many to the right. I just don't have the feel of the flow. But this time I had it just right.

There I was with a 2-shot lead and suddenly I made this beautiful drive nobody could believe. I got so excited about the drive that I hit a 4-iron 20 feet from the hole and 3-putted!

I was lucky, though. The green was real soft from so much rain and it had a lot of footprints on it. Nicklaus hit it in there about 10 feet from the hole and missed it, too. I guess the soft greens bothered him a lot, too. Or maybe he was in shock from seeing me hit that drive. I know I was. Some shots will do that to you.

# BLOWING HOT AND COLD

The coldest weather I've encountered in a golf tournament was not in the British Isles but in Las Vegas, Nevada. When we played the Sahara Tournament on the Paradise Valley course in the autumn of 1971 the temperature was 26 degrees and the wind was blowing off the desert at 35 miles per hour. I was so cold my hair hurt.

I won the tournament after being six shots behind. I've always felt the only reason I won was because I stayed up drinking red wine until four o'clock on the morning before the final round.

Because I was so far behind I didn't feel I had a chance to win, so I spent most of the night going to shows and drinking. I think that's the best thing that could have happened to me, because when I went out on the course that cold blast of air sobered me up and sharpened my senses. I shot a 66, even though I couldn't stand to scratch my ear.

I was wearing all my sweaters and rain gear, trying to keep warm, and I used my umbrella to block the wind. Somehow I still struck the ball very well. I guess that red wine kept me perking.

I also have played in sleet at a couple of unlikely tournaments. One was Jack Nicklaus's Memorial Tournament at Columbus, Ohio. The sleet doesn't seem so unlikely until you consider it was the last week in May. Jack's tournament is a beautiful event, but Columbus can get damn cold in May. I foresee that that tournament someday will be snowed out, even if it's on Memorial Day.

The other time I played in sleet was at San Diego, which usually has beautiful weather and sunshine, even in February. When the front blew in, Fuzzy Zoeller and I were going neck and neck for the lead. We had to delay play for thirty minutes to clear the sleet off the greens, and when we came back Fuzzy beat me.

One of my best rounds ever in the British Open was the 67 I shot on the second day at Muirfield in 1980. There was rain and mist and it was very, very cold. I really don't like to play in cold weather, but I've never let it bother me in a British Open. When I go there I'm a long way from home, I'm spending a tremendous amount of money to make the trip, and I take the weather in stride, regardless of what it may be.

The hottest place I've played is Singapore, where Orville Moody and I won the World Cup in 1969. I made the statement that week, 'It's so damn hot here they don't even have insects.' I meant it. I couldn't find any bugs in Singapore; I guess it's so hot they can't survive. And the humidity makes you feel like you're in a steam bath all the time.

Panama is the second hottest place I've played. It's very consistent. The temperature is 100 and the humidity is 100.

I sweated so much that I never could keep enough liquids in my body. I wore a cap when I played, and it was so soaked with sweat that when I leaned over a putt the sweat actually dripped off the bill of my cap onto the ball. I would back off, get a towel, and dry my cap, but before I could get back to putting it would start dripping again. It was ridiculous.

There were a lot of complaints about the heat at Southern Hills in Tulsa, Oklahoma, when we played the US Open in 1977 and PGA Championship in 1982. It was very muggy but it's not in the same league with Singapore and Panama. Compared to those two, I could have played in an overcoat at Southern Hills.

# A MANNER OF SPEAKING

The British are curious people. Their lingo is different and they certainly have their own way of expressing themselves. Of course, when they hear Americans talk they must think the same about us.

After the second round of the 1984 British Open at St Andrews, Jack Nicklaus was asked at a press conference if he thought he still had a chance to win. Jack answered the question with a popular expression from America.

'Well, you know what they say,' he said. 'The opera ain't over 'till the fat lady sings.'

When a sheet of quotes was distributed in the press tent, that one came out this way: 'Well, you know what they say. The opera is generally not finished until the large woman begins singing.'

One of my pleasures of travelling the world is hearing how people talk in different countries. I find I'm rather good at knowing where some folks live after listening to them for only a short while.

I hear someone speak Spanish and I'm pretty sure whether he's from Cuba, Puerto Rico, Venezuela, Spain, or Mexico. Each has a different dialect. Just as in the United States you can certainly tell if someone's from Boston or Texas or Georgia. In Hawaii, they cut all their words off: 'Hey, bub!'

Although the British Isles are fairly small, I usually know where people live by their dialects. The Yorkshireman sounds one way, the Londoner another, the guy from Wales another. You can damn sure detect the one from Ireland and the one from Scotland.

I was pretty confused by what I heard on my first trip to Britain, however. I played in the Alcan Golfer of the Year Tournament at Royal Birkdale in the autumn of 1968, and I didn't know what my caddy meant when he told me to beware of the 'burn' in the fairway, or to hit my ball toward the 'marquee.' I had to learn that a burn is a creek and a marquee is a tent. And pretty soon I learned that you don't go to the drugstore here. You go to the chemist's.

At dinner one night a guy told me, 'I'll knock you up in the morning.' I did a double take when I heard that. In my country 'knocked up' means somebody gets pregnant. Over here, they're going to call you or come to your door – 'knock you up.'

One night during the British Open in 1971 we were having a big party at the Kingsway Casino in Southport. Everyone had been drinking quite a lot, and some guy walked up to me with a strange look in his eyes.

'I'm pissed,' he told me. I thought he was mad at me and wanted to fight. I was getting out of my chair. But Willie Aitchison, who caddies for me in all my British tournaments, heard it, too. 'Hold it, hold it, hold it,' Willie told me. 'He doesn't mean anything by that.'

'Well,' I said, 'when someone comes up to you in America and says, "I'm pissed," that guy wants to fight.'

Willie grinned. 'All that chap means by "pissed" is that he's drunk, intoxicated, inebriated, or whatever you want to call it.'

'Yeah,' I said, 'I guess he's just drunk.'

The British and I are on pretty familiar terms now, but occasionally I shake some of them up, too.

I have a good friend in England named Jack Aisher. He's chairman of the board of Marley's, which is a British chain of tool-and-supply stores, and he likes to throw dinner parties. One year we were at Gleneagles, having a swell time. Everyone was making toasts, something the British dearly love to do.

'To the Queen!'

'To the Prince of Wales!'

Well, I listened to that for a few minutes, then I grabbed a glass, stood up and shouted, 'To Paul Revere!'

Some huge, fat guy with a walrus moustache started coughing and sputtering, 'My man! My man!' I leaned over the table, patted his shoulder, and said, 'Aw, I'm just kidding you!'

The British say 'bloody' a lot. Hit a bad shot and you'll find your ball in 'the bloody bunker.' Hurry or you'll miss 'the bloody train.' Get caught on the course without an umbrella and you'll get soaked by 'the bloody rain.' Once I got my ear tuned to it, I realized they use 'bloody' as we use 'lousy' in America. Or if they say, 'You bloody well better do it,' that's

like our saying 'you dadgum well better do it.' Dadgum? The British must wonder what sort of bloody expression that is.

While in America we like to call someone of the opposite sex 'sweetheart' or 'honey,' they say 'love.' Jimmy Tarbuck, the comedian, tells the story about a couple out walking their dog when another woman walking her dog falls over the edge of a cliff. The woman was hanging by the heather, and her dress was blowing over her head. The husband stood there and his wife said, 'Love, if you keep looking at her, you're gonna go blind.' And the husband said, 'Well, love, I think I'll risk one eye.'

The Scots have their special sense of humour, too. I like the story about the caddy at St Andrews working for a man who got so upset with his game that he threw down his clubs and said he was going to drown himself in the bay.

'Go ahead,' said the caddy. 'You coudna keep your head doon long enough anyway.'

# STRANGE ENCOUNTERS

I have found myself playing a course for the first time and saying to myself, 'Boy, this is a great golf course.' Then, *bang!* there will be one or two holes that don't even belong there. I mean they're just weird.

One famous one with a flaw is Riviera. You could probably go to Communist China and say 'Riviera Country Club' and some guy would say, 'It's in Los Angeles, California.' It's known worldwide, but Riviera is a *17*-hole golf course.

The clinker is no. 4, the par-3. A monkey's as good as a man playing it. It slopes away from you. It plays against the prevailing wind because the play is toward Santa Monica and the ocean, and the hole plays about 240 yards against the wind. Hell, you have to hit a driver on it. They should plough that damn hole up and start building a legitimate par-3.

Other than that, Riviera is a fine place to play. The rest of the holes are interesting, the kind you want to try your game on. You can tell a good golf course when you remember each hole distinctly after you've played the course two or three times. If you've played it many times and you don't know one hole from another, then you can forget it.

Colonial in Fort Worth is one I always remember. I'd rather play there than anyplace else, even if the club got shafted by the US Army Corps of Engineers some years ago.

The engineers told Colonial it needed some property from the course to stop the Trinity River from flooding. Then they changed two great holes, numbers 7 and 8. Particularly no. 8, which was one of the meanest little par-3s I'd ever seen.

Before, your ball had to carry the river to reach the green, and you had to hit it just right. The green was surrounded by big trees, and if you didn't hit it you'd automatically make a 5 or 6.

It wasn't a long hole, only about a 6- or 7-iron shot, but there was a big bank in front and the green sloped down like a saddle. If you hit the ball on the back of the green it would roll to the front, and if you hit it on the front it would roll to the back. To hit the centre of the green you wanted your ball to land past the flag so it would trickle back down. That was a great test of shotmaking.

Now the Trinity River is exactly where that green used to be and the hole is in front of the water. It's entirely different. It's not the distinct challenge it once was, but I guess the Corps of Engineers is happy.

When I won the 1968 US Open at Oak Hill in Rochester, New York, I tied Ben Hogan's scoring record of 275 and became the first man ever to shoot four rounds in the 60s. Oak Hill then was a very old golf course, with some great holes and some plain ones. But when we played the 1980 PGA Championship, the course was different. The PGA said the course wasn't tough enough and brought in George Fazio, a course architect. Number 6 had probably been the most demanding little hole there ever was, but Fazio rerouted it and ruined it. When he finished, it wasn't even the 6th hole anymore. It was the 5th, because he'd eliminated a par-3 that had been the 5th hole. Then he made another par-3 for the new no. 6, a hole where you can't even stay on the green. The PGA wanted something different, and that's what it got, like it or not.

Some years ago a corporation bought the Pinehurst complex in North Carolina and decided to redo Pinehurst no. 2. That announcement brought an uproar because Donald Ross built that golf course. Man, you don't go in and redo a Donald Ross golf course! That's like painting the Lincoln Memorial orange.

Donald Ross was one of the first architects to bring the old English-Scottish tradition to US courses. He built them tough, but he built them in a way that you could score on them whether you hit the ball in the air or rolled it. Now you don't find a course being built that way in the US. We have elevated tees and elevated greens and they don't have the 'old world' look to them that you find in a Donald Ross course.

Everything was flat on those old courses in England and Scotland because they didn't have earth-moving machinery then to build up tees and greens. You couldn't do all those things with a mule and plough. Donald Ross kept this style and his Pinehurst no. 2 was not elevated nearly as much as most other US courses.

Finally, they decided to leave that course alone except to add some new tees and make it extremely long. That was a mistake, because

Donald Ross built those greens to take a certain shot. Players were hitting 4-, 3- and 2-irons to a green that was built to take a 7-, 8- or 9-iron or a wedge that had backspin on it. A lot of people don't understand that everything is related to the contour of the green, that you build a green according to the length of the hole. They lost this when they lengthened the tees, and that's how they ruined Pinehurst no. 2.

Sawgrass, where we play the Tournament Players Championship every March, has been heavily criticized and for good reason. It's a beautiful layout and it's great for spectators because it's a stadium-type course. But the waste bunkers are too big and in the wrong places on some holes, giving you no fairway to hit, and the greens aren't worth a damn.

I can't understand it because I believe Deane Beman, commissioner of the PGA Tour, and Pete Dye, the architect, really tried to build something different and good. I think they built it too quickly a few years ago, and you make mistakes when you do that. They made it a little too difficult.

The bumps and contours on the greens are just not any good. You can't bump and run the ball. If the wind blows, it blows hard, and you may shoot an extremely high score because you can't get to the green without hitting your ball high in the air. You can't roll it into any of the greens.

I know how bad it can be when you have an off day there. I shot my highest round ever, an 84, on the first day at the 1982 TPC and then withdrew.

I played the back 9 first, and by the time I reached my 17th hole – no. 8 on the front side – I was in terrible shape. The bunkers were so deep they actually used sod to keep the banks up. My ball hit in the bank so I went in the bunker and found it at about eye level. The imbedded-ball rule applied so I dug the ball out and dropped it with no penalty. But it rolled in the bunker where I couldn't hit it. I dropped it again. The same thing happened.

Finally I just took the ball, went on the other side of the bank and sat down. I hit the bank with the heel of my shoe until I made a little plateau. Then I teed my ball up on the plateau and chipped it on the green. Of course, it was totally illegal. First, you can't make a plateau. Second, you can't use a tee for your ball.

The old British courses generally have been good to me. You may see some greens shaped like cloverleafs and boomerangs in the US, but in Britain they usually are round and level. This is because the wind blows so hard that you need to keep your ball low and bump and run it onto the green. The bunkers are so deep that you need a ladder to get inside.

The wind gets so strong on those links courses that if the bunkers were shallower all the sand would blow onto the green.

I had two strange experiences in the British Open on the Old Course at St Andrews in 1970.

I really should have won my first British championship there. I had a 3-shot lead on the final day, but I 3-putted five greens and shot a 77. That was the day the British press made a big deal about my giving the Prime Minister, Edward Heath, a 'wet hand.'

At first, I couldn't figure out what the hell they meant by that. I had had an unexpected meeting with Prime Minister Heath while I was standing on the tee. It was cold, and I spat in the palm of my glove, trying to warm my hands. Just as I did that, somebody punched me in the back. I turned and there was the Prime Minister, holding his hand out to me. I quickly shook hands with him, then hit my tee shot. The next day the headline in the newspaper said, TREVINO GIVES PRIME MINISTER HEATH WET HAND.

Well, I wouldn't give the devil a wet hand. It was all accidental, but the press took off on it. Maybe a lot of people weren't upset, however. Heath wasn't re-elected.

Personally, I would have preferred to win the championship and then to give the Prime Minister my best dry handshake at the presentations.

# THE STUFF OF LEGENDS

The senior golf tour is a real money tree today, but do you know where the seed was planted?

It happened in April 1978, at Onion Creek Golf Club, a course built by Jimmy Demaret just south of Austin, Texas. That's where Demaret and Fred Raphael introduced a tournament called the Legends of Golf. Now there's a proper name if I ever heard one.

The tournament became a tremendous success on television in 1979 when Julius Boros and Roberto de Vicenzo played six extra holes before they finally beat Tommy Bolt and Art Wall for the team championship. It's always a good show, and I'm glad I can be part of it.

NBC covers the Legends of Golf, and it's probably my most enjoyable work of the year as a commentator. These players are so rich in history that you always have something to talk about.

It all began because Demaret and Raphael believed there was a strong national interest in seeing the old champions play in tournaments designed to showcase them. Raphael, who produced a great TV series called 'Shell's Wonderful World of Golf' in the 1960s, had good financial and television contacts. Demaret had all the contacts he needed with the players – and the course.

Onion Creek is a great place for a seniors event like the Legends. It has some hills and trees and a little creek running through it, and it's 6,584 yards long, a good length for older players. Jimmy, bless his soul, never took any credit for developing such a fine course.

'The Lord put it there and I didn't change it,' he said. 'All I did was manicure it.'

Most of the old champions were excited about playing when Jimmy told them that this tournament was limited to those who had passed their fiftieth birthday and that the purse was $400,000. In 1978, that was more money than they were paying at most events on the regular US tours. Sam Snead told Jimmy to count him in. So did Boros, de Vicenzo, Bolt, Wall, Jackie Burke, Gardner Dickinson, and the Hebert brothers, Jay and Lionel. Jimmy even reached way back and got Ralph Guldahl, who won the US Open in 1937 and 1938. And, of course, Gene Sarazen said he would be there, wearing his plus-fours. Sarazen was almost eighty at the time, but he was still game to play.

There would be a lot more good players turning fifty during the next few years. Guys like Arnold Palmer, Don January, Gene Littler, Miller Barber, Gay Brewer, Billy Casper, Peter Thompson, Chi Chi Rodriguez, and Gary Player would make the field, and senior golf, even more attractive. That's why Jimmy and Fred Raphael believed so strongly in the Legends of Golf.

Naturally, it would be even better if Ben Hogan played. Hogan hadn't played in a tournament since 1971, and Jimmy knew how proud his old friend was and how sensitive he was about playing in front of people. But he knew Hogan's presence at the Legends would be the crown jewel.

I remember sitting in the locker room one morning at the 1983 Legends, the last one Jimmy played in before his death, and hearing him talk about Hogan.

'Before the tournament began in 1978, I called Ben and told him there would be a four hundred thousand dollar purse,' Jimmy said. 'He said, "Jimmy, they're not going to pay that kind of money." I called him again and told him the four hundred thousand dollars was definite and talked about our playing as a team. Ben sounded like he was interested, but it never got any further than that. He decided to stay away.

'This year we wanted to honour him even if he wasn't playing. We just wanted him to be present. He didn't want that. That's Ben. He's different.'

Sam Snead is the same age as Hogan but his attitude was exactly the opposite. Sam loved to play even though his eyes and his back weren't as strong as they once were. At the first Legends, in 1978, Sam was sixty-six and he teamed with Gardner Dickinson to win the championship. That was worth $50,000 to each of them. In 1982, when he was seventy, he helped Don January win another championship. By 1984, the senior tour had grown to twenty-six events paying more than $5 million in prize money. I was visiting with Sam at the Legends and asked him how many tournaments he could have won if there had been all this senior action when he turned fifty.

He looked at me under the brim of his straw hat and grinned. 'I would have won 'em all,' he said.

And maybe he would have. Sam won a regular tour event, the Greensboro Open, at the age of fifty-three; he's an amazing athlete. One thing for sure: the years hadn't hurt his confidence.

Just being in the locker room at the Legends and listening to Sam and all those old stars talk is a delight. One day Paul Runyan walked around swinging a strange contraption, a baseball bat with four plastic fan blades attached to the top. 'This is great,' he said. 'Swing this fifty times and you're ready to play.'

Sam was sitting in a large leather chair. 'If I swing that thing fifty times,' he said, 'I'll be ready to come in.'

Gene Sarazen had been busy that week, as usual, being interviewed about the secret to his long life and golf career. 'I eat an apple every day,' he told a Houston writer. Then he told an Austin TV guy, 'I get to bed early, get up early, and drink the right Scotch.' When Paul Runyan swung past, Sarazen grinned. 'If I had you around my house,' he said, 'I wouldn't need air conditioning.'

Another interviewer sat down with Sam to ask some questions. I loved Sam's answers.

'It seems you've taken care of your money,' the guy said. 'Is it true you have a lot of it buried in tin cans in your backyard?'

'Aw, Jimmy Demaret started that lie, and I've never been able to squash it,' Sam said. 'He also told people that's the reason I never bought anyone a drink. Well, why should I help someone carry on a bad habit?'

'Of all the shots you've made,' the guy said, 'is there a special one you remember?'

'Yeah,' Sam said. 'One time at Chattanooga I hit a real pretty iron to the green, and danged if my ball didn't hit a bobwhite in the air and knock it dead. My ball stopped about a foot from the cup and I tapped it in. Only time I ever made two birdies on the same hole.'

These guys have such wonderful memories and they have given so much to golf. I'm sure glad that the Legends of Golf helped them to have a second life in their sport. Liberty Mutual, an insurance company, has sponsored the Legends for years, and the tournament's place is firm on the American sports scene. TV fans always are anxious to watch it, and the gallery at Onion Creek for the final round has reached 35,000.

These guys are treated like visiting royalty and they should be, because these Legends are the backbone of the game we know today. They're the

ones who held the golf tour together back in the days when the purses were small, keeping it alive for guys like myself to come along later and play for big money. Maybe we should show them more respect and call them 'Mister' – Mister Snead, Mister Bolt, Mister Burke – but that's not their style. A lot of us should say thanks for what they did. I'll be glad when I turn fifty and can get out there with them.

# FUNNY THINGS HAPPEN OUT THERE
## (THE SNAKE FINALLY APPEARS)

MY caddy, Herman Mitchell, isn't exactly built for speed. At 5 feet, 11 inches and 300 pounds, Herman is one of those people put together for the long haul. But for one incredible moment at Sawgrass I really believed he could have outrun the world's fastest sprinters for 50 yards.

When it comes to the funniest things I've seen on a golf course, this was in a class by itself.

We were waiting to hit our second shots on no. 2, a par-5, at the 1984 Tournament Players Championship when nature called. Because there are woods on the right side of the fairway and the gallery is only on the left side, Herman decided to slip into the woods without comment. It was clear to me that he'd have to move deep enough into the trees so the gallery wouldn't be able to see him. In a flash Herman disappeared from view, leaving the rest of our group standing on the fairway. The gallery was quiet when Herman came out of the woods. Then suddenly he was in flight. Herman's big feet were crunching branches in his wake and he sounded like Bigfoot crashing through those trees.

And then I heard him scream.

As I looked back I noticed he was running sideways. He broke through three or four bushes and fell to the ground, still screaming. His visor rolled off his head and he scrambled to his feet and took off. I never saw someone that big run so fast.

Herman exploded onto the fairway, his eyes as big as saucers. I said, 'Herman, what's wrong?'

'I stepped on a snake!' he said. He was panting hard and sweat poured down his face.

A marshal asked him, 'What happened to your visor?'

'I left it in there,' Herman said, pointing to the woods.

'Well, I'll get it for you,' the marshal said.

'I don't want that visor,' Herman said. 'Let the snake have it!'

Years before, I had learned that even a toy rubber snake was no joke to Herman. We were on the 18th green at Colonial in Fort Worth and I suddenly reached in my bag and pulled one out that my daughter had gotten at the zoo. I waved it at Herman and he damn near ran into Crampton's Lake. And now he had come across a live one.

I knew Herman was scared. A lot of people would be. But the way it happened and the look on his face were so funny I couldn't stop laughing.

You see, there was a snake, even though it wasn't in a sandtrap.

Another occasional caddy and friend of mine is an American Cuban everyone calls Chico. He takes a Florida vacation from his job as a janitor in New York City every spring to caddy in my pro-am group at the Doral Tournament. He keeps me in stitches, especially when he sounds like the late television comedian Freddie Prinz. After the critical shot he can be counted on to say, 'You're looking gooooood!'

At one pro-am, I hit my tee shot and then the first amateur stepped up. He hit a line drive off the toe of his driver to the right. The ball went about 35 yards into the gallery and hit some guy right in the rear.

The shot really popped him. Pow! The poor guy jumped high in the air. I know it had to hurt, but Chico yelled, 'Yeow!' and started laughing. This started me laughing and then he got Herman laughing so hard he was falling down, holding his sides. It wasn't so funny for the guy who got hit, but it *was* a funny scene. You would have laughed, too, and we chortled over it for nine holes.

Then on the 17th, the caddies were standing in palm trees beside the fairway when one of the amateurs hooked his ball in their direction. We hollered 'Fore!' and they started scattering, but the ball hit my friend Chico right in the seat of *his* pants. That started us laughing so hard again that we almost didn't get to 18.

Maybe there's something about playing golf in Florida that creates funny situations. Once at Arnold Palmer's tournament in Orlando, the gallery had a big laugh when a player hit his ball right beside a big alligator on the 6th fairway. The player didn't think it was very damn funny, though. He asked for a ruling but was told he would have to play

his ball from that spot. The alligator didn't move, and the player couldn't get close to his ball. Finally, a marshal drove a golf cart real close and that alligator went in the water; then the guy hit his shot.

I guess he never should have worried about it. People in Florida say an alligator is so scared of you he won't bother you. But I know one 300-pound caddy who'll never get close enough to find out.

# TV AND ME

I didn't like the contract NBC sent me after I told them I was interested in doing golf commentary on television. It definitely was one-sided. It looked like a Chinese phone book – about five inches thick and full of dos and don'ts for me. What really got me was the morals clause.

This said NBC could cancel me out at any time for shabby behaviour. So I told the NBC people, 'I don't mind the morals clause, but it should be broader. I'd like to have Grant Tinker, the chairman of the board, have a morals clause on him, too. If he does anything I don't like, then I want the right to get the hell out myself.'

I feel morals clauses work both ways. If I work for a company and they do something ridiculous, I think I should have the right to get out and get all my money because they embarrassed me.

NBC realized I didn't want to mess with that contract, so we agreed I should have my attorney draw one up and send it to them in New York. We sent them about two pages covering what I felt was important, and that's how we got together.

I'm glad we did because I had really gotten interested when I learned NBC had hired Vin Scully and that I would be working with him at some tournaments.

I always admired Vin. I had listened to him do baseball on radio, and I knew him from the golf tour when he worked for CBS. I think he's the pro's pro. I liked the idea of sitting beside him in that booth overlooking the 18th green, talking golf.

Still, I was damn nervous at the first tournament I worked, the Bob Hope Desert Classic. That was January 1983; to make it worse, I had pneumonia. After the telecast, people told me, 'That didn't sound like you. You must have changed your voice just for this job.'

I said, 'No, to tell you the truth I was dying up there. I was completely out of my environment. I'm a professional golfer, not an announcer.'

But as I did more tournaments, I felt better. Working with Vin and Charlie Jones, who moves into the booth in the spring when Vin switches to baseball, made me comfortable. Charlie also is a real pro, a guy with a fabulous voice and great knowledge. Once I spent some time with NBC I realized we have a pretty good family out there. Besides Vin and Charlie we have Jay Randolph, John Brodie, and Bob Goalby working on the course. Guys behind the scenes like Larry Cerillo the producer and Andy Rosenberg the director bring it all together and make it work. They told me from the beginning that I should just be myself, to say what I wanted, and NBC would back me 100 percent. I've probably given them some nervous moments, though.

During the Tournament of Champions at La Costa that first year, we were well into the last round and Lanny Wadkins, the defending champion, was winning again. We had taken two different head shots of Lanny, one on Saturday and another on Sunday, to be used during play. Now Lanny was about to hit a shot on the 15th or 16th, and Jay Randolph was talking about the situation. In my ear I could hear Andy Rosenberg talking to me on our private line from the production truck. He said, 'You know after this we're going to lead into that second clip.'

Without even thinking, I said in the broadcast microphone, 'Andy, we did that damn clip yesterday!'

And he shouts at me on the inside line, 'We're on the air! We're on the air!'

For a while I felt like climbing out of that tower, walking off into the Pacific Ocean, and never being seen again. But you're going to make mistakes. If you try to watch every little word you say, you're not going to be natural.

I'm in an unusual position, still being an active player when I'm not working for NBC. Knowing a lot of the players well can help. The second year I worked the Tournament of Champions, I did interviews with Hal Sutton, Lanny Wadkins, and Raymond Floyd. Then NBC asked me to try and get Jack Nicklaus just a few minutes before he was to tee off. He walked up and I said, 'Jack, can I ask you a question on television?'

He kind of whispered to me, 'Lee, I don't do interviews before I play. You know what I mean.'

I said, 'I understand. I don't like it that way either.'

Then he walked about three steps, turned around, and said, 'Okay, for you I'll do it. What do you want to ask me?' That was nice.

But I believe I get respect from these guys because not once have I cut

them up. Instead of knocking someone by saying he's hit a lousy golf shot, I'd say, 'Hey, we hit them like that sometimes, and I'm sure he'd like to have that one back.' I try to give the public what it wants, but I have to remember I have to play and walk and share the same locker room with those players.

People ask me, 'How far are you going with this television career?' Well, this is as far as I want to go. I'm Lee Trevino, not Howard Cosell. That man is a sports genius. He can do anything – football, baseball, boxing. He'd be great doing ice hockey. People who are avid fans think he's too strong with his opinions, but he has tremendous knowledge. I'd like to sit them down with Howard Cosell and go through a quiz on rules, plays, players, and records. He would bury them in a minute; he's a walking encyclopaedia.

Me? I'm just happy doing what I'm doing: going down and interviewing a few players. Saying hello to everyone. Coming on camera and explaining to the audience what's going on. A little smile here. A little smile there. Just talking about the tournament and the people playing it.

I'm not interested in doing football, baseball, track, and any of that other stuff. I'm just a pro from one field who has the pleasure of going into that booth and working with pros from other fields.

# AN OLD
# FAVOURITE

I treasure Tenison Park, which is one of the few places left in Dallas where I had my fun when I was younger. The roller-skating rinks, bowling alleys, movie theatres, and other golf courses are gone, cleared away to make room for new buildings in a growing city. But Tenison Park has survived, and I'm glad.

It may be the most famous municipal course in the world, and I've had something to do with that. But a lot of people are confused about how long I played there. After I won the US Open in 1968 a story went around that I learned to play golf at Tenison as a little boy. The truth is I never set foot there until the summer of 1961 when I was twenty-one and had returned to Dallas after four years in the Marines. But once I did, I knew it was my kind of place.

I had played a lot of golf at Bob-O-Links, another East Dallas course operated by Harry McCommas and his son, Hal, and I liked it there. But Tenison was special. It was only a ten-minute drive from Hardy's Driving Range, where I worked afternoons and nights. Tenison had thirty-six holes that really tested my game. A lot of different people played there and they mixed well together. It was kind of like a big family, and I felt very comfortable. It was always exciting. Tenison had a tremendous influence on my play, and my life. It always will be one of my favourite courses.

It's a rolling layout, with thousands of pecan trees and an old cream-coloured clubhouse sitting on a hill between Samuell Boulevard and East Grand Avenue. Erwin Hardwicke was the pro for years and he was the perfect host. Your background didn't matter. If you could pay the greens fee, you went out and played and had fun.

Lee Elder also played there as a young man, and he was as poor as I was. A lot of wealthy people played there, some for fun, some for big money. Tenison was the only golf course I've ever seen where the parking lot was filled with Cadillacs, jalopies, pickups, and beverage trucks. I had a friend who worked for a bottling company and went by Tenison to play every morning. Then he'd work like hell in the afternoon to deliver those soft drinks.

Tenison was the hardest 'easy' course I ever played. It had only one bunker – to the left of the 18th hole on the east course – but it had such length and such character that it didn't need any. The many trees made it a very difficult golf course. When the US Publinx Championship was played at Tenison, they let the rough grow, and the winning score was something like 13 over par. It has big greens, but it's just so difficult. It was the perfect place to sharpen my game.

Tenison is also where I met Arnold Salinas, who became a great friend and years later joined me in Lee Trevino Enterprises. People in the Pan-American Golf Association told me Arnold was the best Mexican-American player in Dallas while I was in the Marines, and then they told him how good I was. They kept trying to get us together, but I always went to Tenison at six in the morning and he came later. Then one Monday there was a pro-am and we drew each other.

We won, shooting 13 under, and I was low pro. I believe I beat Arnold by a stroke. I asked him if he could play the next morning. He said, 'Look, you'll have to come by and pick me up if you want me on any golf course at six in the morning.'

So the next morning I walked right into the Salinases' house and into Arnold's bedroom, woke him up, and we went to Tenison. I think I woke up the whole family, but no one got mad at me. I guess they just figured I was crazy.

Some wild stories have me winning thousands of dollars gambling on the golf course at Tenison, but it never happened. Sure, there were some very big games, but I didn't have the money to get in them. The biggest bet I ever made in those days was $5, but that's a big bet itself if you don't have a penny in your pocket.

The big-money players were a fascinating bunch of guys. The most famous was Titanic Thompson, but there were plenty more who loved action – Arthur Corbin, Jack Keller, Joe Campisi, and some I just knew by names like Ace and Fat Mickey. And there was Dick Martin, probably the best player I ever saw until Jack Nicklaus.

Dick would have been great on the tour, but he was just a little early. He came from the Ben Hogan era, and I guess the tour, which didn't have big purses then, didn't appeal to him when he could make so much money at Tenison. He was a little guy, only 5 feet 5 inches or so, but he had more shots and was as accurate as anyone I've seen. And he wasn't scared of anyone.

He also was a great creator of games. People congregated around him, anxious to play with him, because he could think of so many ways to bet. Sometimes Dick took a couple of dozen guys out to play in the snow, and they painted their golf balls with Mercurochrome. Sometimes they played with baseball bats.

They had the Tunnel Game, where you put up $25 apiece, took one club, and went out to the farthest point on the course. You tried to hit your ball back to the clubhouse across the front 9 on the east course, but you had to go through a concrete tunnel under the railroad track between the no. 2 tee and no. 1 green. If you hit over it, you had to come back and knock your ball through that tunnel, which was a narrow 40-feet walkway. If a guy didn't put his ball in the right position he might take 12 or 13 getting through it. You could hear some fantastic cussing around that tunnel.

They played one called Honest John, where you paid every other player $10 for each stroke you took. If you had a bad day, you could lose a tremendous amount of money. Another was called Trees: you paid every other player $10 for each tree you hit. At Tenison, with all those pecan trees, that could get pretty damn expensive. And if your ball bounced off one tree and hit another, you paid each guy $20.

Then there were the regular big-money games, where they finally went out and played after sitting in the clubhouse half the day drinking coffee and trying to out-hustle each other. They usually just played nine holes because they spent so much time arguing and bullshitting, trying to get strokes and win the match before they ever teed off.

They played what we called the Cutback on the east course: 1, 2, 3, 4, 5 and then over to 15, 16, 17, and 18. The course could be full and three or four players might be on the 14th hole when you'd see a gang coming down no. 5 – maybe a half dozen of the biggest gamblers in Dallas with fifteen or twenty people following them in carts. Next thing you knew they'd jump over in front of you on 15. No one would dare say anything to them. No telling how much artillery they had under their jackets and in their socks and golf bags.

You couldn't blame them for not getting too far out. There had been holdups way back on the course when robbers took thousands of dollars. There's a great story about one of those robberies. When the gamblers got back on the 8th hole, two guys came out of the trees with shotguns. Before one guy handed over his money, he counted out $1000 and handed it to another victim. 'Here,' he said. 'We're even.'

I got into only one big game with those guys before I went on the tour. That was in 1965 when the Fat Man, Martin Stanovich, came to town. He dropped by Hardy's to offer me a deal. I knew him by reputation, a golf gambler from Chicago who looked for big games.

'I want to go to Tenison and play Dick Martin and some of those other guys,' he told me, 'and I want you for a partner. I'll put up all the money. All I want you to do is to club me and read the greens for me. I know that you're not a big gambler and you don't play with them, so I know you won't put me in the middle.'

I told him he didn't have to put up any money for me, that I'd play with him just for pleasure. Well, we played the west course with Dick, Erwin Hardwicke, Hal McCommas, and two or three others, and he beat them all with my help.

He was a fine player, even if he didn't look like one. The Fat Man was about 5 feet 10 inches tall and 240 pounds, and he wore a big old ugly Panama hat pulled down on the right side like Al Capone. He had the left side up so he could see how to swing, but he looked terrible hitting the ball. He used Croyden clubs with grips twice as long as normal, and he'd choke way down on them. He had a god-awful swing. He held the club way out in front of him, and when he hit the ball he'd fall back on his right foot. But it was a come-on. If you're a golf hustler, you've got to have some gimmicks. You can't look good.

Well, he sure didn't look good, but he could play.

As for me, I never hustled a soul at Tenison. A hustler is a golfer who lies about his handicap. Hell, I didn't have a handicap. I always said I was a scratch player. Of course, I shot 66, 67, or 68, but I didn't call that hustling, just good playing. Besides, who could I find to hustle at six in the morning?

My first wife, Linda, and I were married a few months after I began playing at Tenison. When our son Ricky was a few months old, we moved into an apartment on Shadyside Lane, just across East Grand from Tenison, so I could get to the course sooner. If the weather was hot I wore Bermuda shorts or cut-off jeans, old T-shirts, and sometimes I went

barefoot. If the mosquitoes were biting, I'd go into the creek and pack mud on my legs and arms to keep them off, something I learned in the Marines. I looked like hell. My golf bag was a little $2.95 canvas job with a hole in the bottom, so I carried it on my shoulder like a rifle or across my back. If I had carried it the usual way all of my clubs would have fallen out the bottom.

I would walk across East Grand to the 14th tee on the west course and start playing from there. I could play 18 holes by ten in the morning and have time for more before I went home to shower, eat lunch, and get to work at Hardy's by two. Usually I played with Arnold Salinas, Howard Buchanan, and Bobby Moreland, and, as I said, we never played for much because we didn't have much – a dollar a side, twenty-five-cent skins, and low score taking a dollar from everyone else. If they didn't show up by six-thirty, I'd tee off alone.

I didn't have to have a game. I'd hit two balls, pretending one was Ben Hogan's. 'Ben Hogan' never won a match. His ball always was the one that missed the green or a short putt.

In reality, I did beat Dick Martin quite badly once. I shot 62 on the east course and he was in the game. He was a very smart player, and when he saw I was having an excellent day he quit pressing on 14. I won $100, the best day I ever had at Tenison before I went on the tour.

Later, when I had plenty of money, I'd come back and play three of them – Dick, Erwin, and maybe one of the assistant pros. We'd play $25 automatic one down so I was betting $75 and they were betting $25 apiece. It's difficult to beat three people and I only won once. I lost as much as $1000 on 18 holes, but, what the hell, I had the money. It was fun doing it, with all those people following us. And we were lucky: we never got held up.

# CUP OF CHEER

When the PGA of America named me captain of the United States Ryder Cup team for 1985, I was ecstatic. And it proved how far my knowledge of international golf competition had come.

The first time I made the team was 1969. When they told me, I said, 'What's Ryder Cup?'

But once I flew to England with the US team and played those matches against the top British players, I realized how special the experience really is. It's one of the rare opportunities a golfer has to represent his country and spend the week as a teammate of eleven other players he normally competes against.

Ryder Cup matches are played every other year in September on a home-and-home basis, and I made the team five more times over the next twelve years. I won my share of matches and I was always happy about how the British fans treated me when we played there. I helped to keep the Ryder Cup away from their country, but my wins were very popular with them. I thought I'd love to captain the Ryder Cup team and I'd love to captain it in Britain. And that's why I was so happy I was chosen for 1985, when the matches returned to England at the Belfry in North Sutton Coldfield, home of the British PGA.

As always, we had an all-star team, and I knew exactly what my job was. I'm a good cheerleader. The only thing to do with such fine players was pump them up. I usually can get the best out of people, particularly people I know well. Well, I knew all these guys and they knew I was really behind them.

But I also wanted them to realize how tough it can be. Sure, the US has dominated the Ryder Cup since I was a teenager, but that doesn't mean we have a lock on it. In international competition, the best players are out there representing their country, and they get pumped up, too.

I pointed to the 1984 Davis Cup final as a perfect example. Now, who would have thought Sweden would beat John McEnroe and those guys? McEnroe and Peter Fleming had never been beaten in doubles, but they got dusted. Everyone from the US got dusted.

And you never know when something crazy will happen to mess you up.

In 1969, the British really played us tough at Birkdale. At the end of the third and final day of matches, Miller Barber and I played Tony Jacklin and Peter Townsend. When we came to 18 it was almost dark and we were feeling a lot of pressure. The teams were tied, and the US hadn't lost to Great Britain since 1957. My caddy was Willie Aitchison, a Scot who carries for me when I play in Britain. Willie was good – he once caddied for Tony Lema and Roberto de Vicenzo when they won the British Open – but he talked a lot.

When I got to the tee I looked for my bag and Willie wasn't there. Then here came a guy carrying my bag; I've never seen him before. 'Where's Willie?' I asked.

'He was talking to someone coming up the hill,' this stranger said, 'and he slipped and broke his ankle.'

I still had that on my mind when we reached the green. I missed an 8-foot putt which kept us from winning outright, and that let Great Britain tie us, 16–16. When Willie came hobbling up, I somehow didn't feel sorry for him.

Four years later, when we played at Muirfield I learned my own lesson about talking too much.

You don't know who you'll play in singles until the names are drawn each day, and Peter Oosterhuis was giving us a difficult time. Nobody could beat him. So I sounded off at a team meeting. 'I wish I could draw him. I can beat him.'

Well, the next thing I knew I had drawn Oosterhuis. Unfortunately, I couldn't stop talking. I was so confident that I told my teammates that if I didn't beat him I would kiss each of them in a most unlikely place.

Damn, talk about pressure! The next day I had Oosterhuis one down coming into the 17th, but I 3-putted to square the match. I missed the 18th green and he didn't, so then I really had a problem. He 2-putted, so that meant I had to chip up and make the putt or I'd lose the match.

This was the last match of the day. It was dark and I had the most difficult 8-foot putt I've ever seen in my life. I didn't even look at the hole because I couldn't see it anyway. I just put my putter down in front

of the ball, hit it, and it went dead into the cup. I didn't lose, but I didn't beat him, either.

Back at the hotel I sat down to have a beer and relax when suddenly all of my teammates were standing in front of me with a photographer. Man, I had to talk fast to get out of that one!

Through the years I realized that each captain has his own style. Arnold Palmer was captain at Ligonier, Pennsylvania, in 1975. In Ryder Cup you play thirty-six holes a day, and we were so far ahead before the last afternoon's round that some guys told Palmer they were tired and didn't want to play. I told him to put me in the first match, but before I teed off I enjoyed a lunch of six beers. I lost, 5 and 4, but it didn't matter. I was just out for fun.

After the first 9, we went right by the pavilion. I saw Palmer sitting on the lawn and I screamed at him, 'Hey, Arnold, give me a couple of beers!' So he grinned, grabbed the beers, ran down to the fence, and handed them to me. He was a helluva captain.

Sam Snead was the easiest captain I ever played for. He would start telling us stories in the clubhouse and we'd forget to go out and practise. When it was time for the matches, he came in and asked, 'Well, how are you all feeling?' And we said, 'Great, Sam.' Then we would talk awhile and he would put some players together for a match without worrying about it too much. When you're playing alternate shots, you want to put a long hitter with a short, straight hitter, but Sam put Jack Nicklaus and Tom Weiskopf out there together. They got their brains beat out. They couldn't keep it on the fairway.

The Ryder Cup has such a great tradition in Britain that I have seen from 20,000 to 25,000 spectators on the course each day. When we play in the US we're lucky to draw five thousand. Because it is so important there I believe they made a mistake in 1979 when they changed the makeup of their team and made it Great Britain–Europe.

I had told British officials that instead of bringing in Europeans they should make it a Commonwealth team. I thought it would have been great to bring in some top players from Australia and Canada. But they went against that and I was really shocked they did. This meant they could add some great young players like Seve Ballesteros of Spain and Bernhard Langer of West Germany, but I still believe a Commonwealth team would have been better.

I've always enjoyed being part of it, however. The camaraderie is great. For example, Sammy Torrance of Scotland is a very good friend of mine and in 1981 he gave me a ride to and from the hotel each day, although we were playing each other in matches and I was doing well.

One morning on the way to the course he said to me, 'You know, I think I'll just drive on to London. That way I'll be guaranteed half a point – a double default.' He grinned and then pulled in at the club. I beat Sammy, 6 and 5, that day. He still gave me a ride back to the hotel, though.

# JUDGMENT CALLS

A lot of people knock John McEnroe for the way he acts during a tennis match. He screams and hollers at the official when he thinks he's gotten a bad call, but I think McEnroe is good for tennis.

I was watching him explode on TV one day and someone asked me why golfers never act that way. I told him that McEnroe does it to wake up those line judges. Golf is definite. Either you knock the ball in the hole or you don't. A tennis match can be decided on a judgment call, and McEnroe raises hell with those guys to keep them alert.

How many times have you seen a tennis shot replayed that showed the linesman was wrong? That's why I am leery about what might happen in any sport that has judgment calls.

I've been asked to do some promotional work for the Olympics to raise funds. I told the Olympics people, 'I'll be glad to do that whenever you start curfewing and locking up the officials. Some guy is judging diving and I don't know how much vodka he drank the night before. I don't know what pills he's on. Why don't they give a urine test to the judges, too?'

I'm serious. You have some diver who has worked for years for a chance to win a gold medal, and you're going to let some judge with a hangover give him a number? Same thing in gymnastics or boxing or the long jump. One time Carl Lewis jumped 30 feet and should have broken the world record, but an official ruled it out. He thought he saw Lewis step over the line by a fraction of an inch on his takeoff. Most people thought that official was wrong, but his ruling stuck. That's when a judgment call can blow you away.

If you ever want to see some hell break loose in a golf tournament, just change the rule about putting. Instead of having a cup in the ground, draw a white circle on the green. Then have an official stand there when

you putt at that white circle and decide if your ball caught enough of it to be in or out.

Do you think there would be any fist fights on that green? That's what a judgment call could do to golf.

McEnroe can go on raising hell, as he must; fortunately I can take my sport just the way it is.

# RIGHT IDEA, WRONG COURSE

When Seve Ballesteros and I tried to play the Old Course at St Andrews one day with nothing but a 5-iron, it was a great example of where your mouth and your pride can get you.

Seve was always talking about how good he was at playing an entire round with one club, and I had said that I could beat anyone in a one-club match. We talked about it so much that someone decided we should put this thing together and film it for television.

So there we were, the day after Seve won the 1984 British Open, playing a 9-hole match in front of the BBC cameras. We didn't exactly bring the Old Course to its knees. It was closer to the opposite.

Seve shot 38 and I shot 40. I 4-putted on the 2nd hole for a double bogey and never could make it up. This sure wasn't what we had in mind when we talked about how great a one-club match could be.

The 2nd hole, by the way, wasn't no. 2 but no. 12. Because there was work underway on part of the course, we played the holes that were farthest from the work: 11, 12, 13, 14, 5, 6, 7, 8, and 11 again. On long putts, Seve putted left-handed with the back of his iron. On short ones, he putted right-handed. I putted right-handed all the way and kept wishing we were playing on a flat course.

We just tried this on the wrong course. You can't play St Andrews with your whole set, much less one club. Our scores were ridiculous. On a course with greens that hold and good fairways, we would have shot much lower.

We couldn't make any birdies, and we were lucky to hit any greens because of the undulation. And the ground was as hard as a table. I still think the concept is good. I think people like to see different golf shots, and you're going to have them when you play with just one club. If these are played on the right type of courses, one-club matches can create a tremendous amount of public interest. They also can bring the art of shotmaking back to golf.

Youngsters tend to emulate the players, and if they see us playing matches with one club, they'll start doing it, too. And that's really the best way to learn to play the game. If you're allowed only one club you will have to create a tremendous number of different shots with it. It's the best way for youngsters to learn finesse on the course and to develop a tremendous feel around the greens.

Despite our scores, we had fun with that match.

On the first hole, no. 11, Seve got up and down from the Strath bunker, which I guarantee you is one larger bunker. When we played no. 11 again to finish the match, the BBC crew asked him to hit it out of the sand again for the cameras. He hit his ball up, and before it could roll back I snared it in my cap. After the kind of day we'd had out there, that seemed the best way to end it.

# HEAVY THOUGHTS

If you want to find a model case of a golfer losing weight, don't look at me. I'll bet I've lost 3,000 pounds in the last fifteen years, but I still weigh the same.

I'll go on diets and lose 10 or 20 pounds. Then I slip off them and gain everything back in a week. So don't ask me what my best playing weight is. I don't know. I'm only 5 feet 7½ inches tall and I've never played lighter than 175 to 177 pounds. I might be a helluva player if I ever got down to 160.

Seriously, I really think I would be a better player if I weighed 170. And after reading a book called *Eat to Win*, I began thinking I could get down to that.

The author, Robert Haas, doesn't give you a diet. Instead, he tells you what foods you should eat to have the most strength, the most stamina, and to excel at the top of your capabilities. So I tried his way and I liked it. I fixed a baked potato, but instead of loading it with butter and sour cream, I stuffed it with yogurt and low-fat cottage cheese. It was fantastic – the best baked potato I've ever eaten.

Maybe you better find yourself another model case while I'm working on this. If you really want an inspiration, look at a picture of Jack Nicklaus twenty years ago and look at him now.

In his early years as a pro, Jack's nickname was Ohio Fats. He was bulgy and his crew-cut blond hair made him look worse. Then he called his tailor and made an appointment for three weeks later. Jack said he was going to lose 30 pounds and he would need a new wardrobe.

He did, too. He became much thinner and let his hair grow. He let it get just shaggy enough to be handsome. And he never gained the weight back. Now that's willpower.

David Graham did the greatest job of anyone on the tour in giving up

cigarettes. He smoked two or three packs a day. Then he just stopped one day. That's willpower, too.

Everyone has willpower but they just don't want to use it. Someone says, 'I'd love to quit smoking but I don't have any willpower.' What the hell does he mean, he doesn't have any willpower? Sure he does.

That same person might like to speed down a freeway at 100 miles per hour. But why doesn't he? He has willpower.

I think a lot of people misinterpret willpower. Willpower is something you can apply to everything you do.

Do you want to get up early in the morning? No, but you do. Why? Because you have to. You've got willpower.

So when someone tells you he can't stop drinking or smoking because he doesn't have the willpower, that's a bunch of baloney. He just doesn't want to stop.

I know. I've had times when I didn't want to stop either.

I once said, 'All running does is make a good-looking corpse.' I was just kidding, though. I once did a lot of jogging and I really liked to get out by myself. That was my meditation time and I loved it. But I haven't jogged in a long time and I don't think I will again because I've had so much back trouble. Besides, a golfer doesn't need it.

I don't see anything wrong with a person running if that person has a desk job all day and that's his only exercise. But for a golfer to run is crazy. Not only that: it's stupid. He is on his feet for eight hours a day, either on the golf course, the practice range, or the putting green. Why should he go out and run after all that?

If he's heavy, he's eating or drinking too much. Exercise will not make him lose weight without a proper diet. So he needs willpower.

And if he needs inspiration to start using it, he can just look at those pictures of Jack Nicklaus.

# WINNING BOTTLE

Golfers love gimmick bets, and I'm no exception. The most famous one I ever created was playing with a Dr Pepper bottle, which some people still think I used everywhere I played.

The only place I actually made money with that bottle was at Hardy's Driving Range in the early 1960s, when I worked afternoons and evenings there after playing for hours at Tenison Park. The action was good at Hardy's, too, and between selling balls, running the 9-hole pitch 'n' putt course next to the range, and closing up at night, I found time for some great bets.

The Dr Pepper gimmick started accidentally. I had a family-size bottle, a 32-ouncer with thick glass, and I was fooling around with it at the driving range, throwing balls up and hitting them. I did pretty well so I started practising with it. I broke one and nicked my hand so I came up with a solution. I wore a glove on my right hand and wrapped adhesive tape around the neck of the bottle so I wouldn't cut my hand if it broke. I got better and better with it, so I went to the pitch 'n' putt to try it out there. I knocked the ball on the green, then putted croquet style, crouching and swinging the bottle between my legs. I was good, but I practised with it almost a year before I got into a match. Then I played with that bottle for three years against all comers and their traditional equipment and never lost.

My first match was with a fat little insurance salesman who loved that par-3 course and would not play unless I played with him.

He wore clothes from the Roaring Twenties, always had his hat sideways, and carried a big wad of money. He worked in the poor black and Mexican communities, collecting weekly premiums, and he kept about 300 one-dollar bills rolled up with a hundred-dollar bill around them. He couldn't stand it if he didn't come by two or three times a week to play

me on the pitch 'n' putt and drop $10 or $15 each time. He was a solid loser, this man.

He'd say, 'There aren't too many people who can play like me on this par-three, are there?' 'No,' I'd say, figuring to butter him up and bring him back. Maybe I hustled the guy, but I never stuck a gun to his head. He wanted to gamble. He went for anything. He was a natural for the Dr Pepper bottle.

When I was working I would only play the 1st and 9th holes, the two closest to the clubhouse, so if somebody drove up I could run back and wait on them. He came by one afternoon and said, 'Let's play a couple of holes.' 'No,' I said. 'Hell, you can't beat me.'

'But you know I'm good,' he said.

'Yeah, but you can't beat me with my club.' I hesitated, then I said, 'Hey, I've got a new deal for you. You might have a chance to win. I'm going to play you with this bottle and you give me the ties.'

'What do you mean, ties?' he asked.

'If I tie you on the hole, I win it,' I said.

He grinned. 'You've got it.'

Well, he parred the two holes but so did I, so I won. After that I asked for a half-stroke a hole when I played with the Dr Pepper bottle.

The little guy never could understand it. 'I think I can do that,' he said. 'Let me try.' He'd throw the ball up and whiff it every time. After a lot of practice I had the eye-hand coordination to hit the ball cleanly, but he didn't. So he would go back to using a club and I kept beating him with my bottle.

No matter how often I did it, he just couldn't believe I could win every time. Other people who played me felt the same way, so I cashed in on something I discovered by accident.

I never dreamed it would lead to much bigger money a few years later. After I won the US Open in 1968, there had been so much publicity about me and that old bottle that Dr Pepper signed me to a four-year contract at $50,000 per year. I did television commercials, held clinics, and represented the company at special gatherings. Once, when they had a distributors' meeting in Dallas, I gave an exhibition on the front lawn of their headquarters on Mockingbird Lane, hitting golf balls with that old 32-ounce family-size bottle.

But I had to quit demonstrating that on a regular basis, because they quit making the bottles with very thick glass. I could still take a bottle with thinner glass and hit the balls. But even though I taped the neck of the bottle and wore a glove, the kids who might try this trick could pick up a bottle, forget the tape, throw the ball up, and crash! The bottle could break and cut their hands. I soon realized it was time to stop this little game.

But people never forgot. They still ask me about that Dr Pepper bottle. And somewhere that fat little insurance salesman may still be wondering how I did it.

# WHEEL OF FORTUNE

I have won some big paycheques and collected some fancy fees for many years, but I'll never forget the feeling of being flat broke. That's how it was in the autumn of 1965, when I was out of work and seemingly out of luck. Then a couple of guys named Bill Gray and Martin Lettunich came along with offers I couldn't refuse.

In a moment of anger I had quit my job with Hardy Greenwood at his driving range in Dallas. As my employer, Hardy had refused to sign my application for a class-A PGA card, which I needed before I could play on the US tour. Hardy said I wasn't mature enough to handle the responsibility of travelling on my own all over the country, and later I realized he was right. I had married again the year before and I still was very impulsive, which I proved by quitting my job when our baby girl, Lesley, was only a few months old.

My wife, the first Claudia, found a job as a file clerk for an insurance company, but her pay was only $55 a week. I wasn't playing in any pro-ams. The fact is I wasn't playing anyplace. I went to Tenison, but I never had any money to bet so I would just hit practice balls – maybe two thousand a day.

Then one bright, spring day Bill Gray came to me and offered me a great deal. Bill was about my age, a bachelor who loved to gamble. We'd known each other around Tenison a long time, and he knew what I could do on the golf course. 'I'll sponsor you,' he said. 'We'll go to Houston and you can play in the Texas State Open. I'll pay expenses and give you sixty percent of what you win.'

So we drove down there and I entered. Clyde, Claudia that is, went too, and we stayed at the Tidelands Motel, which I thought was the fanciest place I'd ever seen. The Texas State Open had a pretty good field, with players like Homero Blancas, Gay Brewer, and Bobby Nichols. Bill Gray got busy betting and I played real well. I beat Frank Wharton in a play-off and won $1000, which was the most money I'd ever seen in my life. I cashed the cheque, Bill gave me $600, and we came home happy. He'd killed 'em betting, and because I looked so good in the tournament I was invited to play in the Mexican Open in November.

Bill Gray was living high then. He bought a new Oldsmobile Cutlass and drove us to Mexico City, where I finished second to Homero Blancas and won $2100. I was excited but I didn't have any money to throw around. I had been out of work a long time and we owed plenty – rent, furniture, doctors, insurance. Still, some surprising things had happened, and all of them were good for me.

Like a phone call from El Paso. Before we went to Mexico City, Clyde and I went to a movie one night while her mother, Lou, stayed with Lesley. When we got home Lou told me, 'A man named Don Wilson wants you to call him in El Paso.' Don Wilson played the tour a little and did some hustling, which is what he was doing out there. He was calling me from Horizon Hills Country Club and he told me a guy named Martin Lettunich wanted to talk to me.

'I don't know any Martin Lettunich,' I told Don Wilson. But, they were paying for the call so I decided to talk to him. Later I learned that Martin Lettunich is a wealthy man and a really good guy. He farms thousands of acres of cotton at Fabens, outside El Paso; he has cattle and he's on the board of two or three banks. And he loves to gamble.

So Martin comes on the phone speaking Spanish. '*Hey, chico, como está todo?*'

I said, 'Wait a minute. I may be Mexican but I don't speak Spanish that well.'

So he said, 'Well, let me tell you what I've got here. I asked Don if he knows someone who can play this game, and no one knows it, and he said, "Yeah, I know one guy, Lee Trevino from Dallas." Well, we're playing a little golf out here and want to know if you can join us for a couple of days.' One of the guys he wanted me to play was Fred Hawkins, who was famous for finishing second on the tour.

We were planning to leave for Mexico City in four days, but when Martin Lettunich said he would send me a roundtrip airline ticket, pay my expenses, and give me $300, I couldn't catch that plane soon enough.

I took an early-morning flight to El Paso, and Robert Sparks – wearing a cowboy hat and driving a pickup – met me at the airport. I'd played golf with Robert in Dallas, and his mother owned a lot of land north of El Paso. He took me out to Horizon Hills, and I looked at the course and played a few holes real quick. The other players would start descending on the club at noon, but Martin Lettunich came early to have coffee with me.

I had a silver golf bag with *MacGregor* and *Lee Trevino* written on it. Probably the greatest thing in the world for a young player is to have a bag with his name on it. I was really proud of that thing. But when Martin saw it he said, 'Oh, no, chico, we can't have that bag.' He went in the storeroom, found a little tattered bag with the bottom falling out, and put my clubs in it. 'Use this,' he said. Then he took me out to hit practice balls before anybody showed up.

In a little while Fred Hawkins stopped by. Well, I was as nervous as a dog eating razor blades. He was the bridesmaid of the tour, and there I was wearing a raggedy old shirt and pants, with mud all over my shoes. But that was how Martin wanted it. He told me he didn't want me to look good. Then another player, Gene Fisher, showed up.

He introduced me as his tractor driver. 'This little kid's been practising,' Martin said, 'and I think he can beat y'all.' Then Hawkins and Fisher started hitting balls, and I was on the putting green when Frank Redman appeared. Frank was a top amateur player, and once it was a toss-up in El Paso as to who would go on the tour, he or Hawkins. He also had been a USGA official for years and knew a lot about what was happening throughout golf.

He stopped Hawkins and asked, 'Fred, who are you playing today?'

'I don't know,' Hawkins told him. 'Some little Mexican boy out there on the putting green that Martin brought in here.'

Redman took one look and said, 'Do you have any idea who that kid is? That's Lee Trevino from Dallas. He just won the Texas State Open. Fred, that kid can lay it down.'

Well, Hawkins wasn't impressed. 'If I've never heard of him,' he said, 'he can't play.'

I ran right over Fred Hawkins those two days, shooting 65 and 67. Martin Lettunich and his friends made a killing betting on me, and he was one happy farmer when he gave me the $300 and put me on the plane to Dallas. When I landed, Claudia and Bill Gray were waiting at the airport with the car parked. We headed straight for Mexico City.

When we got back from the Mexican Open, Bill and I were excited about taking off again, this time for Panama, Caracas, and Bogotá. We

picked up our passports, packed up Bill's Olds Cutlass again, and headed south. We believed we'd have no problem driving to the Panama Open. Bill had put his fingers on a map and said, 'Lookie here, from Dallas to Mexico City is this far, and we drove it in a day and a half. Mexico City to Panama City is about the same distance. We'll be there in three days.'

Well, let me tell you something: there ain't roads all the way through. It took us eight days to reach Panama City, and every damn thing went wrong. We went through Guatemala, Honduras, El Salvador and Costa Rica and didn't have visas for any of them, so we spent hours and hours doubling back to the appropriate consulates where we could get the necessary papers. Even though we drove through riverbeds and the densest jungle I'd seen, they looked a lot better than the hotel in El Salvador where we stayed one night.

We were in a huge room, sort of a dormitory with blackboard partitions separating the beds. It was so hot that I opened a window and then fell asleep. Next thing I knew, there was something on my bed and Bill was slapping at it. I turned on the light and saw it was a huge bat! I jumped up and killed it with my putter and we got out of there. We slept in the car the rest of the trip.

One time in the jungle we were stopped by a little blockage in the road, and a guy came out of nowhere. He was wearing khakis and carrying a submachine gun. I said, 'Oh, goddamn.' If he wanted the car or anything we had, he could have killed us and thrown us out. Well, I tried to be friendly. In my broken Spanish, I said to him, 'How you doing?'

He glared at me a minute, then said, '*A donde van?*' (Where are you going?) I said we were going to Panama to play golf.

He walked around the car, his hand on that machine gun. Then he said, '*Cigarro?*' (Cigarette?) I gave him a whole carton of Parliaments! Then he vanished as quickly as he appeared and we took off.

We stayed at the Panama Hilton and I won $500 or $600 in the tournament. Bill's car was a shambles, so we left it there and flew the rest of the way. I was sitting on my luggage in the hotel lobby, waiting for him on the night we were to check out, when he dragged in after an all-night party. He had spent every nickel we had, but we managed to pay the hotel bill with a credit card. When we wound up in Bogotá, I won $600 or so, but he blew that too. He kept bailing us out with that credit card and finally got us two airline tickets to Dallas's Love Field. His mother picked us up at the airport and took me home. When I walked in the door I had been gone a month and I didn't have a cent to show for

it. My wife and baby daughter were practically starving, and it was almost Christmas. I didn't know what I was going to do.

Then Martin Lettunich called.

'Remember that boy, Gene Fisher, you met when you were out there?' he asked me. 'He thinks he can beat you.'

I said, 'No, there ain't no way he can beat me.'

And Martin said, 'Well, he thinks about it so strong that he's already made a contract with me to play you on five different courses on five different days. I want you to come out here again.'

He paused a moment and said, 'Let me ask you something. Are you working there?'

'No,' I said.

'Well, why don't you just pack up your wife and your little girl and your belongings and move to El Paso?' he asked me.

'Martin, I don't have a quarter,' I told him.

'Don't worry about it, chico,' he said. 'We'll find something for you to do.'

And that's how I wound up moving to El Paso, where I stayed for twelve years. When you spin the Wheel of Fortune, you sure can be surprised where it stops.

# WILDEST LITTLE CLUBHOUSE IN TEXAS

If you ever have driven across Texas, you know how different one area of the state can be from another. Take El Paso. It looks as much like Dallas as I look like Jack Nicklaus. It has mountains and desert and the spirit of an old frontier town. In a way it still is, sitting way out in west Texas, smack on the border of Mexico and New Mexico. And it's an awfully long drive from Dallas – 650 miles. Hey, that's halfway to Los Angeles.

But I was really excited about making the trip in February 1966 when I loaded my wife and our baby girl into my '58 Oldsmobile and left Dallas. We had sold our furniture for practically nothing, put a few belongings in a rented U-Haul trailer, and hitched it to the car. I had $50 in my pocket and that was it. All I had waiting for me was that series of matches Martin Lettunich had arranged with Gene Fisher and the hope of finding a club job that would help me get my class-A card and join the tour. Because I was leaving nothing in Dallas, that was plenty.

When we rolled into El Paso that first day my car was wheezing and we didn't know where we were going to stay. Thanks to Robert Sparks and his mother, we wound up renting a two-bedroom trailer house by the maintenance barn on their ranch. Once we were settled there, I took off to meet Martin Lettunich.

We had an agreement to play five different courses, starting with Coronado Country Club. Gene Fisher, who wanted to play me, was a good golfer, and he turned out to be a good friend. We had a tough little time of it that day. My partner was Jesse Whittenton, who had played defensive back for the Green Bay Packers and now was operating Horizon

Hills Country Club with his cousin. Gene Fisher had a kid named Steve Summers, a pretty good player for the University of Texas at El Paso. We beat them one up and won $400. Next day we went to Horizon Hills.

It turned into a big blowout for us. There were automatic presses – meaning the bets were doubled on each hole – and to this day I don't know how much was won or lost, but it must have been a lot. The wind was blowing 30 miles per hour and the dust was flying and tumbleweeds were rolling across the fairways. I shot 65 and Jesse helped me on three holes, so we had 62 best ball. Gene Fisher shot 81 and the kid shot 79 and their best ball was something like 75.

The next day we were supposed to play at the country club in Juárez but they didn't show up, so the deal ended after two matches.

But I had come to stay. I needed a place to practise, play, and work toward my class-A card. That turned out to be Horizon Hills, where Jesse and his cousin Donnie Whittington really didn't need a club pro but came up with a job for me. Martin Lettunich had talked to Bill Eschenbrenner, the pro at El Paso Country Club, and a lot of other guys in the local PGA chapter, and they got busy trying to help me with the technicalities involving my card.

At first, Jesse and Donnie hired me as sort of a handyman around the club, but my main job was to open at five in the morning, which was good because that was all I wanted to do. My salary was $30 a week. I had time to practise and play all day, and some days I'd win $30 or $40 extra. The only problem was my car had broken down and we lived four miles away. But I just got up at four and jogged to the golf course.

Jesse and Donnie spelled the family name differently because their fathers, who were brothers, never got along when they were young. So Jesse's dad changed the spelling. Jesse and Donnie were barely making it with the club when I came there, having taken it over from the Horizon Corporation, a real-estate-development outfit based in Tucson. Horizon Hills is located about twenty miles east of El Paso, on Horizon Boulevard off Interstate Highway 10. It's up in the sand hills, and is a relatively easy course with no trees. It's 7,000 yards, but you could hit a ball 240 yards and it would roll another 100 on that old hard sand. It had been a public course, a place popular with railroaders and Border Patrolmen as well as the well-heeled cotton farmers, but Jesse and Donnie converted it to a private club and were selling memberships for a $25 initiation fee and $12.50-a-month dues.

There was nothing fancy about it: a very small clubhouse located in the corner of an L-shaped motel. We had only twenty carts and no shed for them so we always charged them outside the pro shop. A lot of players brought their bags on pullcarts. I still remember the sound of those pullcarts with the noisy tyres when people started showing up to play early. They pulled them across the parking lot to the pro shop: *squeach, squack, squeach*! I could tell who was pulling each one from the sound of the cart.

Life at Horizon Hills was the wildest damn thing in the world. There was a tremendous amount of gambling going on. We had some great games with those cotton farmers swarming all over the course, their pockets stuffed with money. Sometimes you'd see a hundred-dollar bill blown against a tree and a gang of them would be hurrying down the fairway. We played with six, seven, and eight in a group a lot of times, but we played fast. They came out there to play thirty-six or forty-five holes a day.

They wouldn't even pay any attention to my little two- and five-dollar bets. We'd go in the bar and settle up and I'd just sit there while Martin Lettunich, Gene Fisher, Leo Collins, Gene McCardle, and those guys counted out fifty- and hundred-dollar bills. Then somebody would say, 'Okay, chico, how much did I lose to you today?' I'd get $15 from one, $10 from another, $5 from another and go home happy. They would too.

These guys confined their drinking to the bar, but we did have four members who loved to booze it up while they played. They'd drink maybe five martinis each before they teed off. Then they drank all around the course and drank some more when they came in. They'd get bombed, four of the funniest guys I ever met.

They never could play in a tournament because they were always drinking, so we came up with a special tournament for them. We called it the Holiday Open and they loved it. They came all dressed alike: white shirts, knickers, knee stockings, and those little French hats with the little balls on top – berets. Two gals dressed in gold tights drove their booze cart around the course, and it took them about seven hours to finish. We told the other players, 'They're just having fun. Go around them.' They came in drunker than skunks and no one had broken 100. We awarded four identical trophies, all inscribed, WINNER, HOLIDAY OPEN. And one of the guys had a tyre mark up his back. He'd fallen down in the middle of the fairway swinging at his ball and another guy had run over him with a cart.

I still had a year to go to earn my class-A card, and Bill Eschenbrenner

encouraged me to play in as many local tournaments as possible. I also qualified for the US Open at Olympic in San Francisco in June of 1966 and finished fifty-fourth. That didn't do much for me, but playing in all those matches around El Paso did.

Martin Lettunich and Gene McCardle trained me to get ready for those. I played from the blue tees and they'd play from the ladies' tees, and they kept the pressure on. They both were 8-handicappers, and I'd play their best ball. We'd play for $10 to $25 a man, automatic one-down presses. If I didn't shoot under 66, I'd lose.

Other days we'd play a $5 Nassau and work on my short game. I had to miss every green with my second shot, then chip it. You think that isn't some practice round? I wasn't wasting any time out there.

One of the toughest matches I ever played was against Bill Eschenbrenner and Frank Redman at Coronado, where I shot 62 and lost to their best ball. We came up with all types of games. We had the $5 Bogey game. If four guys were playing and one bogeyed the first hole, that guy then had to pay each other player $5 a hole until each one bogeyed a hole, ending his part of the bet. Once I played for almost two weeks without a bogey.

In the summer of 1966, after I had played that US Open at Olympic, one of the funniest things happened at Horizon Hills. I was in the pro shop one afternoon and the coach of the Clint High School golf team, a guy named Mark Smith, Sr, came in real excited. 'Hey, Lee, Gene Littler is in the bar, giving my kids autographs, having a few drinks, and telling some great stories!'

I knew that wasn't right because Gene Littler's never taken a drink in his life, he doesn't go in bars, and he's never going to tell any stories. 'Mark, you gotta be joking,' I said.

He said, 'I guarantee you it's him. Go look for yourself.'

I walked to the door, looked at the guy across the room, and came back. 'That ain't Gene Littler,' I said.

'The hell it ain't!' Mark said. 'He's already bought three or four rounds of drinks.'

Well, the drinking and storytelling went on for two hours, and then this guy called for the bill, which was about $150. 'I'll be right back,' he told everyone. 'I've gotta get my wallet outta my car.' So they all sat there talking, and the next thing they saw was that car going down Horizon Boulevard. That was the last they saw of 'Gene Littler.'

# STRANGE SHOOT-OUT

A couple of months after Titanic Thompson visited Horizon Hills, we learned that he had gone back to Dallas and started talking up the action at our little club. And when Ti made a pitch, he could excite people like a carnival barker.

I was working around the clubhouse when Fat Mickey, one of the big-money guys from Tenison Park, walked in. After listening to Ti, the Tenison people sent Fat Mickey out as advance man to set up a match for Raymond Floyd.

Raymond was in his early twenties then – a big, blond, good-looking kid with a wonderful touch – and one of the great young players on the tour. He was living in Dallas and he hung out at Tenison when he wasn't on the tour. Raymond really loved those money games.

The most difficult thing in the world is to handicap a pro playing against amateurs, but the guys at Tenison had some exotic methods. They came up with gimmick games for Raymond to play, like hitting two tee shots and then playing the worse one. 'What do you think you'd shoot?' they'd ask him.

He'd play a hole by having to play his worse ball twice. If one ball was on the green and one in the bunker, he played two out of the bunker. If one putt went in the hole and one went 20 feet past, he putted two from 20 feet. If he sank one putt and the other went three feet past, he putted two from three feet. I've never seen too many pros who could break 40 for 9 holes playing this way.

Raymond also played a lot at Tenison betting his best ball. He'd usually bet he'd score about 62 or 63. He'd do it sometimes, but he lost more than he won. It was just something to do and Raymond liked the action. He was a bachelor then and he lived fast. He was game for anything, just the kind everyone at Tenison liked.

Fat Mickey was a gambler and sort of a small-time bookmaker. He died a few years ago, and the story was it happened in a dice game in west Texas when he got very excited and almost got in a fight. But the day he walked up to me he had a big smile on his face.

He said, 'Hey, these farmers out here like to play golf, don't they?'

'Yeah,' I told him.

'They sure like the way you play, don't they?'

'Yeah.'

'They'll bet on you, too, won't they?'

'Yeah.'

'You think they'd bet on you if we brought Raymond Floyd out here to play?'

'Yeah, if we played my home course.'

I got real interested then, because the toughest thing in the world is to play a professional on his own home course if he's a good player. He knows every club. He knows every blade of grass. He knows every break in the greens. He knows the texture of the sand. And desert greens are the toughest to putt on simply because there is no constant way the greens will break. If you're playing on an ocean course, everything goes toward the ocean. If you're playing in a mountain region, you look for the highest mountain and everything breaks away from that. But in flat desert a putt on one hole will break east, the one on the next hole will break south and the next will break west. I liked my chances against Raymond Floyd.

Fat Mickey stayed that night and talked to Martin Lettunich, Gene Fisher, and some other guys. He played some poker and lost a few dollars to them. It was strictly a setup. He thought he had found a gravy train. Martin told him, 'Yeah, bring the boy out. We'll arrange something.'

So two days later Raymond Floyd drove up. I'd never met Raymond, and I got a cart and went out to pick up his golf bag. I carried his clubs into the locker room, put them in a locker, brushed his shoes, cleaned them and polished them.

Raymond asked me, 'Well, who am I supposed to play?'

'Me,' I said.

He looked at me. 'You? What do you do?'

I said, 'Well, I'm a combination everything. I'm the cart man, shoe man, clubhouse man, and pro.'

He gave me a funny look and then he went in to have breakfast with Fat Mickey and Ace and some other guys from Tenison.

'What time do we play?' he asked.

'One o'clock,' Fat Mickey told him. 'You wanna go look at the course?'

Raymond said, 'Naw, I'm playing this boy here. I don't need to go look at any golf course.'

Raymond put down some of his money, too, and the betting must have gotten pretty heavy. I know those cotton farmers tossed hundred-dollar bills around like most people treat one-dollar bills, and they wanted to bet more on me than the Tenison crowd could cover. I really was under pressure. If I lost, the club would go under.

It was the funniest sight in the world when Raymond and I teed off. There were a bunch of pickup trucks bouncing down the fairway, full of guys drinking beer and watching our match.

Well, the first round Raymond shot 67, I shot 65, and I beat the hell out of him. When we finished we still had a lot of daylight and Raymond said, 'Let's go another nine.'

I said no and he got mad. I told him, 'Look, I can't play another nine. I've got to put the carts up, clean the clubs, and all that stuff.'

He said, 'I can't believe this. Here I am playing a cart man, a bag-storage man, and I can't beat him.'

So he went in the lounge and started playing cards. Raymond was really kind of a wildman then, restless for action. Woodie Bean and Robert Sparks talked him into going dove hunting, and they took off in a pickup with some shotguns. They hunted till sundown, drank a lot of beer, and didn't shoot a single damn dove.

The next day Raymond told me, 'I ain't never going dove hunting with those crazy bastards again.'

'What's the matter?' I asked.

'They shoot at everything,' he said. 'We were sitting on the ground and there weren't any doves around and I had my hat about two feet from me. One guy said, "Aw, hell, there are no doves. Let's shoot something." And he shot my hat!'

Now Raymond never was one not to go anyplace and try anything. So when it got dark the guys said, 'Hey, let's go to Juárez, see some women, drink some booze.'

I don't know if they did it purposely to get him all messed up for the next day's match, but Raymond said, 'Let's go.' So they put up the shotguns and drove over to Juárez.

'My God, we went in all these places with all these women,' Raymond told me, 'and I didn't know what the hell was going on. I had five thousand dollars on me, so I stuck it in my underwear. I didn't know what those boys were up to.'

They stayed in Juárez all night, but Raymond came out the next day ready to play. By now word had gotten around that Raymond Floyd was at Horizon Hills and the crowd picked up. Everybody made the same bets and we teed off. I shot 65 again and he shot 66. Again he wanted to play another 9 and I couldn't play because I had to put those damn carts up. So he went in and played blackjack.

I didn't know how long Raymond was going to stay, but he came out a third day and beat me on the front 9. He shot 31 and some of the guys pressed on the back 9. I shot 30. I'll never forget it: I had an 8-foot eagle putt on the last hole and he had a 6-foot birdie putt. If I made my eagle and he missed his birdie I would beat him for the third straight day.

We both missed. That's when he got his clubs, shook my hand, and said, 'I can find mu-u-uch easier games than this. I have had enough.'

Since that day Raymond has won a lot of money and a lot of tournaments, including the PGA and the Masters. And whenever we meet, we always remember when we first played together in El Paso.

That's why there was a special feeling during our final round in the 1981 Tournament of Champions at La Costa. I had never won a tournament in California, but I knew I had a great shot at this one if I could handle Raymond. I led by 1 when we teed off that morning.

I shot 34 on the front 9, but Raymond shot 33 to tie me. We had a 7-shot lead on the field, so on the back 9 it became strictly match play. It was like old times at Horizon Hills when the cotton farmers bet on me and the Tenison crowd had their money on Raymond. I was watching what he was doing and he was watching what I was doing. It was fun because Raymond and I always have had the utmost respect for each other.

I saved myself with a 25-foot birdie putt on 12 when he was standing there waiting to make a 4-footer, then he hit into the highest rough on the course on 13 and wound up with a bogey. I left an 8-iron four feet from the hole for a birdie, so I walked off 13 with a 2-shot lead. After he bogeyed 15, I felt I had it under control. The three closing holes are extremely tough ones, but I wasn't scared of bogeying all three and I doubted he could birdie more than one.

Raymond and I shook hands when it was over, but this time all I had to do was accept the trophy and a cheque for $54,000. Somebody else put the carts away that evening.

# THE PREZ

I have played a lot of golf with Jerry Ford, first when he was President of the United States and in the years since. He's a delightful man and he absolutely loves to play, but I'm just glad he never handled foreign policy the way he hits his tee shots.

If he had, all of us might be speaking Russian now.

I loved it when he and Tip O'Neill, the Democratic Speaker of the House, played together. President Ford would hit one into the gallery and we'd holler, 'Fore!'

Tip O'Neill would wince and say, 'Be careful, Jerry! You're going to hit a Democrat.'

Then Tip O'Neill would hit one 30 feet and President Ford had a big laugh. As a Democrat and a Republican, they were political rivals but they're good friends. They're intelligent people. They're not feuding like the Hatfields and the McCoys. Whenever I've been on a golf course with them, we just had a lot of fun.

Jerry Ford has a sense of humour and actually he has a pretty good golf game too. He's bothered by those bad knees he's had since he played college football, and he's not able to turn his body the way he'd like. I think he would be an excellent golfer if he had a little chance to turn on the ball. You'll notice that he stands mostly flat-footed when he hits it. Most of his swing is from the waist up.

He has helped a lot of tournaments raise money for charities by playing in pro-ams. He must do twenty of these a year, and he also hosts his own tournament at Vail, Colorado – the Jerry Ford Invitational – which is a great experience for everyone who plays in it.

He is so absorbed in his game that sometimes he is determined to try an impossible shot. Like Jack Nicklaus said, 'He doesn't know he can't hit the ball through the trunk of a tree.'

He's the same man he was when he was President, but it's more

comfortable out there with him since he doesn't have all those Secret Service agents around him. Before, if you went into the woods to look for a ball, the trees moved with you.

Bob Hope is an old friend and he loves to needle him about his wildness. Once he introduced him at the Byron Nelson Classic in Dallas as 'a man whose tee shots have created several new subdivisions.'

He lives most of the year in Palm Springs, California, now, and that's a golfer's heaven. Because there are a couple of dozen golf courses nearby, Hope said, 'Jerry Ford never knows which one he'll play until he hits his first tee shot.'

He takes it all in good humour, though, and even makes fun of himself in his speeches. He told one big crowd, 'I deny allegations by Bob Hope that during my last game I hit an eagle, a birdie, an elk, and a moose.'

It's fun to be around him, but just be sure you stand back when he pulls out his driver.

# PRINCE OF A GUY

Of all the royalty and heads of state I've been around, the one I feel most comfortable with is Prince Rainier of Monaco. We played together in the pro-am when I was invited to the Monte Carlo Open in 1984. I lost my nervousness as soon as I met him on the practice tee.

He's a husky man, maybe 5 feet, 8 or 9 inches tall and about 200 pounds, and he has a good golf swing and a nice personality. When we stood there hitting balls and talking, I would have figured him to be just another player in the field if I hadn't known who he is – he's that natural.

Maybe it was because he was married so long to the late Grace Kelly and visited the United States often, but he's quite American in his mannerisms. We went to his condominium by the course after the pro-am, and there were no servants around. He opened me a beer, poured it for me, and we just relaxed and talked golf.

He's kind of like Fuzzy Zoeller. He likes to needle every once in a while. But that's okay. He's fun, and you feel he really likes your company. He's not doing it just to look good in the eyes of his people.

He has a dry sense of humour that can slip up on you. One night during a cocktail party at the palace, he asked my wife, 'Do you want a cigarette?'

'Sure,' Claudia said.

'Watch out,' he told her as he opened his case. 'I laced it with marijuana. It's my private brand.'

Prince Rainier drives himself everywhere he goes. He has a Rolls-Royce, but I never saw a chauffeur when he drove to the club each day. No sign of security either. He just seems to move about his little country with complete freedom.

Monaco is a beautiful place with the palace overlooking the Mediterranean but it's so small it doesn't have a golf course. We had to go over to France to play the Monte Carlo Open on a little course built up on a mountainside.

I could see the course from my hotel room in Monte Carlo, and it looked no more than 300 or 400 yards away. When you drive there, though, you go up a mile on a steep, twisting road. 'The big problem with having a tournament up here,' Prince Rainier told me, 'is the fog. When it settles in, we just can't play.'

He was right. Two rounds were cancelled because of fog, so it was a 36-hole tournament. But the nights were still great, with the casinos glowing and all the special entertainment for the tournament.

During a show at the royal dinner, dancers appeared on the stage with smoke drifting up around them.

'Are those guys or girls?' Prince Rainier asked Claudia.

'I think they're guys,' she said.

'Well,' he said, 'you know you never can tell these days.'

That's how he is. He enjoys a wisecrack and a good time. I felt comfortable with the man because I could look in his eyes and watch him smile and tell that he is very sincere. He wants to talk to you, and he feels comfortable in what he's doing. He simply is a very warm individual.

And he serves great beer, too.

# THE KING AND I

When I flew home from Morocco with that jewelled dagger the Royal Moroccan Golf Federation presented me for winning its tournament, I had one regret. I hadn't met King Hassan.

Billy Casper had told me about the King and what an avid golfer he became after Claude Harmon, the pro at Winged Foot in New York, had taught him to play. King Hassan had built a 9-hole course on the palace grounds, had it lighted for night play, and hired a club maker to move there from England to do nothing but make clubs for him.

It sounded like it would be fun to meet him, but Morocco was having troubles with some neighbouring countries during the tournament and he had to forget about golf for a while. But a couple of months later I had a long distance call from Butch Harmon, Claude's son, who was the golf director at the royal course in Rabat and who played a lot of golf with King Hassan. Butch said the King wanted to invite me to fly there and play golf with him.

That was a helluva long trip to play a round of golf, but it was what I wanted to do. So pretty soon I was back in Morocco, not knowing just what to expect.

The trip before had been a great experience, even if I couldn't remember making my acceptance speech at a gala after the tournament. We had played on a beautiful course designed by Robert Trent Jones, located in a forest of cork trees, which made it so quiet it was downright eerie. If your ball hit a tree, you never heard it; the cork absorbed the sound.

At the gala there was a lot of dancing and wine drinking while they passed my beautiful jewelled dagger from table to table for everyone to see. An official of the federation told me that I would be called on later in the evening to make my acceptance speech.

It must have been much later. When I woke up the next morning I had no idea what I had said or if I had said anything. Then everyone started complimenting me on my speech, so I figured I had done all right.

Now I was in Morocco again, waiting to play golf with the King. And waiting . . . and waiting.

Three days passed and I was about to give up on our game when the palace called. The King wanted to play the next day.

When they drove us through the gates to the palace I noticed the guards immediately locked them behind us. Butch Harmon explained they always did that when King Hassan was coming out on the grounds. In a minute I saw a clean-shaven man, a guy about my height but thinner, come out of the palace with a couple of Shetland ponies and some dogs following him. This was King Hassan, who also loves animals.

As he walked over to the pro shop by the course, all the ministers and generals and colonels lined up to greet him. The King held out his right hand as he passed, and each one kissed the palm and then the back of his hand and backed off. By now I was feeling very nervous. He was getting closer and closer to me.

'Butch,' I said, 'what the hell do I do?'

'Nothing,' Butch told me. 'Just stand there.'

When the King came to us, Butch introduced me. 'Ah, yes,' King Hassan said, 'It's a pleasure having you here to play.' He was very nice but I still felt jittery.

This man really plays golf in style. He stepped into a little building that had one chair in the middle of the room with a hundred pair of golf shoes lining the walls – all his. Someone slipped a pair on him to match his clothes, then backed away. We were ready to go to the first tee.

The King and I were playing Butch and a colonel who was a good player. He hit his shot about 200, 220 yards, a pretty good shot. Then I got up to hit mine. I took a waggle and shuffled my left foot. My club wouldn't go back. I shuffled that left foot again. My club still wouldn't go back.

Finally I pulled up, looked at the King, and said, 'Your Majesty, I've won the British Open, I've won the US Open, I've won the PGA, and I've won tournaments all over the world, but I ain't never been this nervous in all of my life.'

He started laughing, 'Ah, don't worry about a thing,' he told me. 'Just go ahead and hit it.'

We played seven holes and I birdied five of them, but I kept remembering what Butch had told me: 'Whatever you see him do wrong, don't

say anything. He's not only King, he's the religious leader. He corrects himself.' Well, I wasn't about to do anything.

The 2nd hole was a par-3, and it didn't look like it was 140 yards. I said, 'Butch, how far is this?' And His Majesty said, 'Hit a five-iron.' So I hit a 5-iron, even though I had to take about 40 yards off it. My ball hit on the green and the King smiled. 'Nice shot,' he said.

The 3rd hole was a long par-4, and I was on the fairway looking at about 175 or 180 yards to the green. I said, 'Butch, how far is this?' And the King said, 'I think that you hit a seven-iron.' Well, I booted it like a 5-iron and hit a hook that put the ball on the green for another birdie.

The King really was pleased. I don't think he understood how tough it was for me to do this. But he was very pleasant, a very nice host. And he certainly doesn't want for anything when he's on the golf course. He had three or four sets of clubs with him and a couple of caddies. He had servants walking right down the fairway, carrying trays of water, soft drinks, and food. The King is a chain smoker, and because he is royalty he isn't supposed to throw his cigarette on the ground like we do. A guy stood nearby and each time the King got ready to hit the servant walked over and took the cigarette with a pair of little tweezers. The King would hit his shot, then come get his cigarette out of the tweezers.

The King played good golf. He made some pars. When we finished, he told me, 'I enjoyed this very much.'

I said, 'The pleasure is mine, sir.' And it was.

They set up tables for lunch for everybody on the grounds, but the King was going to have lunch with his wife in the palace. Before he left, he said, 'Mister Trevino, would you like some champagne?' So we sipped champagne and then he went into the palace, and that was the last time I saw him.

I had travelled halfway around the world to spend maybe two hours with him, and I'll always remember it. Maybe King Hassan will remember how he helped me with my irons.

# THE LEMONADE GIRL

I've enjoyed drinks all over the world but there never has been one quite so special as that cup of lemonade at the Hartford tournament in 1969.

I was walking along a narrow road where players and gallery crossed to the 16th tee at Wethersfield Country Club. It was a hot day, and I saw a lemonade stand in front of a house and some kids selling it as fast as they could pour it. Then I saw a small girl standing before me.

She had bright red hair and was wearing sandals and coveralls turned up to the knees. She held out a cup and smiled.

'Would you like some lemonade?' she asked.

I looked down at her and said, 'Well, little girl, thank you very much. What's your name?'

'Claudia,' she said.

'Well, that's my wife's name,' I told her.

At the time she didn't know. This was Claudia Bove and her father, Albert Bove, was the assistant pro at Wethersfield. She knew a lot about golf and the people in it. We chatted a moment while I finished the lemonade, then I headed on to the tee. It was one of those nice little things that happen sometimes. She was eleven years old and I looked at her as a daughter. I couldn't imagine that some day she would be my wife.

When I finished my round, I saw her again. She was hanging around outside the clubhouse and I was getting in my car. I represented Dodge then and I had a beautiful bright red Charger. It had my name right under the door handle and there was a telephone in it.

We talked some more and she told me she lived in town. Her cousin lived in the house by the course where they had been selling lemonade.

She was really impressed by the phone. She had never seen one in a car before.

'Do you want a ride?' I asked her. 'I'll take you home. You can call your mom on this phone and tell her I'm bringing you.'

She shook her head and said she couldn't go, so I left. When Claudia got home later, she told her mom, 'Lee Trevino was going to bring me home, but you told me not to get in a car with anybody.'

Her mom wasn't impressed. 'No, that wasn't Lee Trevino,' she said. 'That was probably some Puerto Rican trying to pick you up.'

'No, Mom, I know it was him,' Claudia said. 'He had his name under the door handle and he had a phone in his car.'

Claudia's father died not long after that. He was in his early forties but suffered from a heart disease that also took his brothers at about the same age. I remembered that little red-haired girl, and each year when I went to the Hartford Tournament I would give tickets to Claudia, her mom, and her two brothers.

Some years later, I took a couple of friends to dinner in Hartford and invited Claudia and Bobbie, her mom, to join us. Claudia was twenty or twenty-one then and going to college. We had a nice visit but the only time I saw and talked to her family was when I went to Hartford for the tournament. My wife at the time, Claudia – or Clyde as she was nick-named – also met young Claudia, and they became fast friends.

That's how it went for the next few years. Claudia became a stewardess for United Airlines and was having fun, travelling all over the country. Once she came to Dallas, dropped by our house, and borrowed a car to drive to Oklahoma to attend a wedding. Two days later, she came back, dropped the car off, and took a cab to the airport.

Then in the autumn of 1982, I got hit by lightning again. I had no idea that Clyde had visions of getting a divorce until she told me one day. That summer we had moved into a big house on Strait Lane in North Dallas, a place into which I'd sunk a ton of money. I thought we were happily married, and not just because of the fancy house.

Once I realized Clyde was serious about leaving me, we agreed to use the same lawyer and settle everything as quickly and smoothly as possible. I got the house after the divorce was final, but in the meantime Clyde continued living there with our younger daughter and son. I moved into an apartment, and Lesley, our seventeen-year-old daughter, lived with me.

During this time I heard that Claudia had a job with American

Airlines, and had been transferred to Dallas. Even though I hadn't seen her in a long time and my life was in some turmoil, I thought about her and how nice it would be to get together again.

Naturally I was concerned about everyone touched by my divorce, especially Clyde and our children. To get through a divorce isn't easy. Also, there was a new golf schedule coming up, and I had to clear my head for that. Who knew what the future held?

I didn't see her for some time after that. I went to California for the start of the 1983 tour. It was on Friday 14 January, the second round of the Los Angeles Open, that Clyde was granted the divorce. I had that on my mind and almost missed the cut. But on the back 9 I told myself I had to get my head together and play golf. I birdied the last 2 holes and made the cut by 1 shot. Then I shot 67 the next two days, tied for 12th and won $5700.

I left LA with money in my pocket, but my heart was empty.

A few weeks later, I was back in Dallas and, without a moment's hesitation, I contacted Claudia. After taking her out a couple of times, I thought about my priorities and decided I didn't want to live alone. I wasn't out looking for someone either. I just knew I enjoyed Claudia's company. She was twenty-four then and I realized I'd known her, however fleetingly, more than half her life.

Claudia enjoyed my company, too, and we saw more and more of each other. There was a great difference in our ages – about eighteen years – but as time passed we realized we wanted a life together. We agreed on what we wanted from life. We talked about our future at some length, then we made our decision. What had started as a chance friendship had grown into a special love.

We studied my schedule, and agreed on a date. On 20 December 1983, we were married in her hometown, not too far from where she once offered me a cup of lemonade.

She's quite a girl. Claudia is independent. She doesn't need me to pamper her everywhere we go. She's intelligent. She can go anywhere and feel comfortable talking about anything – politics, golf, whatever. She's happy-go-lucky. She can go fast; she can go slow. In one sense she's like a chameleon. She just blends into the surroundings, but she's tough and she's very much her own person.

She has a great sense of humour – most of the time. I've called her Clyde a few times but she didn't find that very amusing. So I call her Peep, for Little Bo Peep. She's 5 feet, 1 inch tall and 104 pounds with a tiny waist. She calls me Choo Choo – that's the name of the little dog in the first reader in Mexican schools.

I've given her a lot of credit for inspiring me to play back to championship form, and she deserves it. When we married I had been playing very erratically for two or three years. I had had back surgery twice since being struck by lightning during a rain delay at the Western Open in 1975, but my back still bothered me. Finally, my doctor told me I must quit practising, hitting golf balls seven or eight hours a day. He said standing in one place so long, bent over like a snake, put too much pressure on my back. He said if I just hit a few practice balls before playing, then walked around between shots to stay limber, I wouldn't have back trouble.

That puzzled me. I told Peep, 'I don't think I can play if I can't practise.'

She laughed. 'You've been playing thirty-two years,' she said. 'You don't know how to play yet? You can play on experience alone.'

That's what I've done and I've played some of the best golf of my life. Score one more for the Lemonade Girl.